Report on
THE
JOHN
BIRCH
SOCIETY
1966

Report on

THE
JOHN
BIRCH
SOCIETY
1966

by Benjamin R. Epstein
and Arnold Forster

New York

RANDOM HOUSE

Contents

Foreword

In the early months of 1960, the Anti-Defamation League of B'nai B'rith began to note a resurgence of organized activity on the Far Right Wing of the American political spectrum. We have long been sensitive to developments on both extremes — Left and Right — because experience has shown that these are major areas for anti-democratic activities, religious bigotry, racism and narrow nationalism.

In light of recent events, we have chosen to do this publication because of the immediate challenge presented by the rapid growth of the Radical Right. This study of the John Birch Society seeks to alert all Americans to the alarming drift toward total extremism and its consequent potential of anti-religious, anti-racist and anti-democratic doctrines. Before dealing with the Birch Society, a short comment on the background of the Radical Right movement should be included.

The new extremism, which soon came to be known as the Radical Right, was, in fact, a reappearance of an older manifestation. In the middle 30's, it appeared as the Coughlin Movement, flowered into the reactionary America First Movement, and ended suddenly when the Japanese attacked Pearl Harbor. In the early 50's, it reorganized itself, its guise somewhat changed, and became known as "McCarthyism." After nearly five years of controversy, the American people forced it into oblivion, unfortunately only temporarily.

Slowly it re-emerged as the Radical Right. For nearly four years, the ADL watched it, issued periodic reports and, at the end of 1963, decided the situation was serious enough to warrant full exposure. Benjamin R. Epstein and Arnold Forster, two of the ADL's top executives, thereupon undertook to organize the accumulated data into a carefully documented report. Almost a year later, in October 1964, they completed their study, and Random House issued it as a book called "Danger on the Right."

Many Americans believed that the stern rebuke the national electorate administered to Barry Goldwater the following month in the 1964 presidential election spelled the death knell once more of Right Wing extremism in our country. Unfortunately, they were wrong. In truth, the 1964 campaign period served as the Radical Right's great opportunity to organize its following more effectively and to unify itself more solidly. They used it well.

In the period since November, 1964, the John Birch Society has emerged as the strongest of all Radical Right organizations — as will be shown in the ensuing pages. This was evident in ADL's continuing scrutiny of Right Wing extremism. The authors of "Danger on the Right" therefore decided to reduce the agency's findings once again to a readable report for interested Americans. This publication is the result.

The next few years will, in large measure, determine the exact importance historians assign to the Birch Society. For it is in the years that lie immediately ahead that the American people will be meeting the Birch Society's challenge to American democratic life.

But it is now — in the present — that the Society has thrown down the gauntlet. It has challenged every one of us. It has challenged the processes and the resolves of our democratic republic. It has challenged the orderly progress of this nation toward a deeper understanding of social justice for all men. It has challenged the moral integrity of each and every American citizen.

History shows that America has survived the extremist challenges of the past — starting with the Salem Witch Hunts three centuries ago — but not without national pain, temporary damage, and certainly not without deep and sometimes violent conflict.

Extremism follows patterns — in the emotional nature of its appeal, in the paranoid style of its propaganda, in the semi-secret apparatus it seeks to establish, in the admittedly dirty tactics it employs, in its eventual divisive effects and in its ultimate danger to the Republic.

The American Communist Party fits just such recognizable patterns, as does the now seven-year-old John Birch Society. In fact, the extremist patterns evident in Robert Welch's organization actually parallel the earlier, but ideologically-opposite, Communist Party USA. These patterns inevitably reveal a broad monolith, a controlled apparatus, a utilization of radical philosophy — all observable in American Communism a generation ago, and now seen, once again, in the John Birch Society. These features are obviously useful operating techniques for any aberration of the Left or Right seeking to achieve a base of political power.

The Birch Society urges its members to infiltrate respectable national and local organizations. And the Birchers have insinuated themselves into organized conservative movements in the way that Communists once moved into liberal groups. Like the Communists, the Birchers have set out to change national political thinking and have publicized their intentions.

The Birch Society is part of a dissident phalanx of self-avowed patriots that bores from within, contemptuous of the very democratic processes and safeguards which are its own protection. This is the contingent which cries "traitor" at respected national leaders in Washington, and which in the local town tells a school teacher to "burn in hell" because of her views. This is the organized cadre that spreads accusations of treason by anonymous telephone voices. This is the collective agitator that can tear apart a political club, a church organization, a labor union, or a whole community — as it can tear apart a whole nation.

The Far Left, to be sure, contains a dimension that finds no counterpart in the current Far Right: a deliberate intention that its propaganda activities serve the interests of a foreign power. Organizations of the Radical Right — particularly the John Birch Society, always claim a loyal, patriotic, "Americanist" character for their program and propaganda.

It is this claim which suggests the basic question our generation must answer: Considering its political philosophy, its monolithic structure, its semi-secret membership, its divisive tactics and its radical goals — is the John Birch Society truly American?

DORE SCHARY
National Chairman
Anti-Defamation League of B'nai B'rith

Strength, Growth and Thrust

1

The middle of 1964 to the present has been a period of continued growth and expansion for the American Radical Right in general and for the John Birch Society in particular. In the seven years since it was founded at Indianapolis early in December, 1958, the Birch Society has emerged as the spearhead of the Radical Right. It is the only group on the Far Right which is permanently organized all across the country at the grass-roots level. It alone plans now to spend a million dollars a month.

Among the major organizations of the Radical Right, only the John Birch Society has a nationwide paid staff of organizers and public relations men, a membership active and activated, a permanent recruiting program, a tightly controlled and generally efficient centralized direction, and a financial income which enables it to continue to expand its nationwide organizational structure.

Starting from scratch at the beginning of 1959, the Society has grown to a membership of about 80,000 in some 5,000 chapters across the country, and at the end of 1965, was pushing toward the 100,000 mark. Since 1963 its membership has almost doubled; its cash income more than quadrupled.

The 80,000 membership, directed by Founder Robert Welch from the Belmont, Mass., headquarters of the Society, just about equals the membership of the Communist Party when the Communists were at the peak of their strength in the United States in 1944. The Society is, in fact, a movement and a propaganda and recruitment "apparatus" on the Far Right that is comparable to the Communist "apparatus" on the Far Left in the 1930s and 1940s. The earlier movement of the Radical Left preached Communism while today's Birch Society, on the Radical Right, claims to preach anti-Communism. But in terms of organizational concept, structure, and tactics, the similarities between the two operations often appear more persuasive than the differences.

Infiltration Tactics

The Birchers, like the Communists of 20 and 30 years ago, are burrowing their way into the fabric and the grass-roots of American life and it is already clear that it will take a major effort by responsible forces to root them out.

· The overwhelming majority of Birch members still conceal their membership in the Society.

The Birch Society today has spawned scores of front groups, formed to lure unsuspecting Americans into the Birch orbit and to ripen them up for eventual recruitment into the Society by enlisting their support for limited and high-sounding causes with whose slogans, at least, few would disagree.

· The Birchers have already infiltrated the American political party structure and in some areas have secured footholds at the precinct level and a measurable degree of influence in various arms of the political party apparatus.

Like the Communists, the Birchers have been establishing local book stores all across the country which serve as distribution centers for Birchite and other Radical Right propaganda, as gathering places for Radical Rightists, and as focal points for Birchite activity, much as Communist bookstores in the 1930s and 1940s served a similar function.

The Birchers have available a large stable of speakers, ready, willing and able to travel anywhere in the country to address local meetings, sponsored not only by Birch groups, but by local civic, political and service organizations as well.

Like the Communists, the Birchers have set up their own publishing house and are not only pumping their own books and pamphlets into the nation's ideological bloodstream, but are reprinting the propaganda of like-minded Radical Rightists for wholesale distribution to their own network of bookstores and to bookstores operated by other Far Rightists as well.

Cell Structure

The Birchers are organized into small units designed to operate as isolated islands, impervious to penetration by outsiders. The Communists called these units "cells"; the Birchers call them chapters.

The Birch membership is supervised and directed by paid professional organizers, set up on an area, state and local basis. These professionals were called "organizers" by the Communists; the Birchers call them "coordinators."

Like the Communists, the Birchers get their official "line" from a central headquarters. The Communists got their "line" from Moscow, via National Party headquarters; the Birchers get their line from Founder Welch via Birch headquarters in Belmont.

Like the Communists, the Birchers brook no deviation from the "line." The Communists expelled deviationists; the Birchers do the same, careful as always to refund pre-paid dues on a pro-rata basis.

(Bircher applicants abjectly fill out a membership form that is a resignation signed in advance, agreeing when they join that the Society can drop them at any time and without any necessary explanation for doing so.)

Like the Communists, Birchers are urged to take an active role in political and community organizations. For instance, Robert Welch, in 1960, urged his followers to join their local PTAs at the start of the school year, to get their "conservative friends to do likewise," and to "go to work" to take the PTAs over.

An Ideological Cadre

The Birchers seek to accomplish their purposes by enlisting the support of a dedicated, zealous, disciplined and thoroughly-indoctrinated ideological cadre of workers — distinctly a minority in their areas of operation, whether local, regional or national.

The Birch Society is not designed to mobilize anything close to a majority of the American national population. Like Lenin, Robert Welch of the John Birch Society believes that

3

a dedicated minority, which knows what it wants, can move mountains.

The Birchers' target is the American mind. Like the Communists, their aim is to change — and eventually to control — American political thinking. Their ultimate goal is political influence and political power.

The Communists of two and three decades ago pointed to the growing and — to them — extremist activities of Big Capital. According to the Communists, Capitalism, then in its "last stages," was evolving into fascism and imperialism. In the same spirit, Robert Welch analyzed, in mid-1965, the development of the forces against which he has allegedly aligned his Society:

"(1) The Communist conspiratorial apparatus is now closing in, with every conceivable pressure and deception, on all remaining resistance to the establishment of its police state over our own country; (2) the only existing force that has any possible chance of preventing the completion of these Communist plans is The John Birch Society; (3) we have no chance of stopping and reversing the long patient progress of this conspiracy except — exactly as stated in the Blue Book six years ago — by measures which are *fantastic* enough to be *realistic* in proportion to the danger . . ."

"Fantastic" measures — some of them admitted by Welch to be "mean and dirty" — have become the trademark of Birch Society activity. And the wheels now are spinning. The active search for new members, after an initial policy of quiet recruitment, has been pushed with increasingly high pressure since 1963. All during which time the Birchers have worked to clean up their public image while Welch engaged in some hard-headed planning for future political influence.

Membership

The membership "explosion" that has vastly increased Birch membership rolls since the 1964 national political conventions was the result of many factors. Most of them were related to the Presidential election campaign in which Birchers and other such extremists were active, welcomed, defended and, to a certain extent, triumphant. At the Republican convention, the Birch Society covered itself with a

4

kind of respectability. Birchers misused the campaign as a vehicle to spread their own political propaganda and to recruit new members.

Many Americans were swept into the Birch ranks on the emotional tide of the campaign period. Many others joined after Election Day, when the frustration of defeat made them ripe for recruitment and when the Birch Society's post-election appeal to this group was summed up in the simple slogan: *"Now* Will You Join The John Birch Society?"

From August through December, 1964, the Society set new membership records and early in 1965, the growth was described by a jubilant Welch as having been of "geometric" proportions.

In 1965 membership growth continued, even though other factors were at work. For example:

● Many who joined during the exciting days of the 1964 campaign found the Society demanded too much of their time, energy and dedication. They either drifted away or were dropped from membership by the Society itself, for like the Communists, the Birch Society does not tolerate "dead wood" for long.

● Some of the 1964 recruits — especially Goldwater enthusiasts frustrated by the defeat of their champion — found the Society too radical for their basically conservative viewpoints. They walked away along with still others who found it too "moderate" or too "educational."

Those who remained faithful to Welch's leadership as 1965 turned to 1966 were, for the most part, the zealous, the dedicated, and the indoctrinated — eager to carry out the monthly instructions sent to them by Welch from the Society's headquarters in Massachusetts.

The California Reports

The Birch Society continues to distribute (in packets designed for the indoctrination of prospective members) the report of a 1963 investigation by the California Senate Fact-Finding Subcommittee on Un-American Activities. It found the organization to be neither secret, subversive nor anti-Semitic. Apparently because of the wide circulation of this 1963 report by the Birch Society, a second report was issued by the same committee in 1965. For understandable reasons,

5

it has been ignored by the Birch Society.

The more recent report found that Robert Welch's organization "has attracted a lunatic fringe that is now assuming serious proportions" and has been "beset by an influx of emotionally unstable people, some of whom have been prosecuted in the courts for their hoodlum tactics in disrupting meetings, and heckling speakers with whom they disagree."

The committee's 1965 report concluded:

"We are more critical of the Society now than we were then for the reason that it has, in our opinion, merited such criticism by reason of its activities exemplified by the irresponsible acticles by a member of its National Council, the re-publication of "The Politician," the inexcusable actions of its minority of irresponsible members, and a dangerous increase of anti-Semitism among a minority of the membership."

The members of the Birch Society are believers in the "conspiracy theory" of history and in *absolute political truth* which they alone claim to possess. It is through the Conspiracy Theory of recent American history that fear is aroused — fear, the essential ingredient of extremist strength. The operating premise of the John Birch Society, like that of the Communists, is that over all of our lives and over all the events of our time, there rules a powerful and protected Establishment, perpetuated by a secret conspiracy of vast dimensions. To the Birchers it is Communism — by which they mean the "establishment" of the last thirty years, including the American Government, whether controlled by Republicans or Democrats, whether directed by liberals or conservatives.

To each extreme, whether of the Far Left or the Far Right — to each "out" the other is "in."

The John Birch Society has grown in direct proportion to the growth which its Founder sees in the power and influence of "the enemy." Welch has said his organization's chances of success in saving the country increased from 1 in 10 in 1958 to 1 in 4 today. Yet, paradoxically, he and his Society claim that in the same period, "Communist influence and control" in the United States increased from 20-40% in 1958 to 60-80% today.

6

2   *The War Against Civil Rights*

The major development in the John Birch Society's centrally-directed program during 1965 was the launching of an all-out drive against the civil rights movement.

The assault started in May, with the publication of a pamphlet by Welch himself which laid down the ideological line. Five hundred thousand copies of a 16-page document called *Two Revolutions At Once* were distributed to the Birch army across the country — 100 copies to every Birch Society cell.

In mobilizing his troops, Welch made it crystal-clear that the campaign upon which they were embarking was the single most important undertaking of the John Birch Society in its entire seven-year history.

"Fully expose the 'civil rights' fraud," said Welch in May, 1965, "and you will break the back of the Communist conspiracy."

In *Two Revolutions At Once,* Welch set forth his view that the Negro civil rights movement in America was part of a world-wide, Communist-dominated, anti-colonialism revolution that used the slogans of freedom, independence and self-determination. At the same time, he said, it was part of the Communist-led revolutionary movement against capitalism in the United States itself.

In his analysis, Welch likened the Negro rights movement in the United States to various "national liberation fronts" in Asia and Africa which in his view have been sparked by Communist terror tactics. He claimed that Algeria's "murderous guerilla band . . . given the high-sounding title of the 'Federation of National Liberation'— or FLN" was merely "a preview of what the NRM — the Negro Revolutionary Movement — will do to the people of the South."

7

Old Communist Booklets

The relationship between the allegedly Communist-led national liberation movements abroad and the Negro Revolutionary Movement in the United States was revealed, Welch said, in a booklet published by the American Communists in 1928. Called *American Negro Problems,* it referred to the Southern Negroes as "virtually a colony within the body of the United States of America," and called for the establishment of a "Negro Soviet Republic" in the South.

In fact, this 37-year-old Red propaganda line was repudiated by the Communist Party's 1959 convention — because it had already died in the Red failure to win the American Negro to the Communist cause.

The Birch Society, nevertheless, continues to distribute thousands of copies of the 1928 Communist booklet to support its theme — that the efforts for civil rights equality and for racial desegregation are Communist-inspired and subversive.

Another Red booklet — published in 1935 and entitled *Negroes in a Soviet America* — is also being distributed by the Birch Society. It was originally reprinted by the National Economic Council under its late founder, Merwin K. Hart, a well-known American anti-Semite. Before his death a few years ago, Hart was the leader of Birch Society Chapter 26 in New York; his publications were recommended by Welch to Birch Society members in its early days.

In the June *Bulletin,* Welch said:

"Our task must be simply to make clear that the movement known as 'civil rights' is Communist-plotted, Communist-controlled, and in fact . . . serves only Communist purposes. So let's keep our own activities and efforts concentrated on this central undertaking."

He added:

"Make yourself as much of an authority on the whole 'civil rights' segment of the total conspiracy as you can. We are asking for, and counting on, a very heavy concentration of effort by our total membership during the next few months, to support our belief that the *Civil Rights Drive* and the parallel *Negro Revolutionary Movement* constitute the most vulnerable point for attack. . . ."

Ideological Weapons

There were many weapons which Welch mobilized for the ideological warfare against the civil rights movement to which he had committed his propaganda army. For example, there were published materials. One was a book published by the Birchers' own Western Islands Company. It was written by Alan Stang of the Birch stable of writers, was called *It's Very Simple,* and was essentially a popularized version of the Welch ideology on the Communist character of the civil rights movement. The book had an initial printing of 100,000 copies and sold out in the first few weeks. An additional 200,000 were printed soon thereafter, and more were on order as 1965 drew to a close.

Stang wrote that America's race problem and the effort of the civil rights movement to end it were both planned by the Communists, built up by the Communists and, most important, conducted by the Communists. Describing the Negro movement as a "social revolution" aimed at destroying capitalism, and the Civil Rights Act of 1964 as a major step toward a Washington dictatorship, Stang concluded his polemic by declaring:

"I accuse the Rev. Dr. (Martin Luther) King of being in effect one of the country's most influential workers for Communism and *against* the Negroes . . . I accuse President Kennedy and President Johnson of knowing this but nevertheless, not only closing their eyes to it, but lending a hand. I therefore accuse them both of having betrayed their oath of office."

There were also printed flyers (suitable for use as full-page newspaper ads) asking "What's Wrong With Civil Rights?", followed by: "The answer is, nothing! But there is a great deal wrong with what is being done today in the name of civil rights."

Birch ads declared that the Negroes' problem was exaggerated, that the civil rights movement was not simply "infiltrated" by Communists, but actually "created" by them. Birch postal cards were distributed. One showed Martin Luther King at the Highlander Folk School, in Tennessee, which the Birchers and Radical Rightists have branded as a Communist training school. (King appeared there briefly on Labor Day weekend, 1957, to make a speech.)

9

Another postcard pictured a man identified by the Birchers as the founder of the civil rights movement. They described him as a Hungarian Communist who used such names as Joseph Pogany, John Schwartz, Joseph Lang and John Pepper. They said he arrived in the United States in 1922 and in 1928 wrote the pamphlet, *American Negro Problems,* which laid down the Red line for establishment of the Negro Revolutionary Movement. Aside from the dubious Welchian history, the drawing of Pogany-Schwartz-Lang-Pepper was reminiscent of some of the viciously anti-Jewish caricatures that appeared in *Der Stuermer* during the Nazi era in Germany and of similar caricatures that have been circulated in anti-Semitic ideological circles in the United States.

These recent materials were added to the arsenal of anti-civil rights propaganda which the Birch Society had been using for some time. Its "Civil Rights Packet" already included *Color, Communism and Common Sense* by the late Negro ex-Communist, Manning Johnson, and Welch's *Letter to The South* which first appeared some years ago. Also available were various reprints, all hewing to the Birch line that the civil rights movement is a Communist manifestation, lock, stock and barrel.

The TACT Committees

The campaign for this nationwide attack was created by Welch in July, 1965, with a proposed new and major approach to exposure of the "fraud" known as "civil rights." He called for "the setting up throughout the country of hundreds of local or regional *ad hoc* committees for the specific purpose of telling the truth about the civil turmoil." Anticipating that they would come to be known as TACT — Truth About Civil Turmoil — he gave the shorthand name his blessing.

TACT front groups sprang up and swung immediately into high gear, distributing literature, holding meetings, sponsoring lectures by American Opinion speakers, buying full-page ads in local newspapers, and peppering the letters-to-the-editor columns with Birch propaganda exposing the "truth about civil turmoil."

Welch's choice of the Communist-style front-group technique worked admirably. Many non-Birchite rightists and conservatives were lured into making common cause with the Birchers against the civil rights movement. In many localities, even the newspapers and other media of public information were at first unaware that the TACT committees were Birch fronts. For example:

• In Fort Wayne, Ind., the *News Sentinel* reported the formation of the local TACT Committee and merely noted that it had "been formed to provide information about past instances of civil turmoil in order to prevent recurrences." There was not a hint in the news report of the TACT group's real sponsorship.

• In the suburban Glenview-Northbrook area of Chicago, where a TACT Committee was formed, the local newspaper reported that the committee chairman had said "that the group, conservative in nature, is not connected with any organization." Yet the group's own newspaper advertisement was signed: "The TACT Committee of Northbrook & Glenbrook Division of the John Birch Society."

But the TACT Committees around the country were not the only fronts spearheading the Birch Society's ideological warfare against Civil Rights:

• The "Detroit Committee for the Prevention of Civil Disorder" listed the same post office box number as the local Birchite "Support Your Local Police" organization, and the same individual was listed as chairman of both.

• In La Puente, Calif., "Citizens for the Support of Law and Order" seized on the Watts riots in Los Angeles, in the Summer of 1965, to distribute a flyer captioned "Now Will You Believe?" It was, in effect, an advertisement for Stang's book and bore the "Support Your Local Police" emblem.

• A woman in Whittier, Calif., received a letter from the "Committee for Better Understanding" which listed a post office box in racially-troubled Selma, Ala. The letter ended with: "Yours for less government, more individual responsibility and a better world"— the slogan of the John Birch Society.

While waging war against the civil rights movement, the John Birch Society has, at the same time, diligently sought to create a public image of itself as friendly to Negroes. A

11

mainstay of the Birch Speakers Bureau during 1965 was Mrs. Julia Brown, a Negro lady who had once been a Communist and later an informant for the government. More recently, the American Opinion Speakers Bureau listed conservative Negro newspaper columnist George Schuyler as one of its lecturers. Birch spokesmen go out of their way to make it clear that the Society has Negro members. As part of the campaign to rid itself of any anti-Negro stigma, the Society has established a Manning Johnson Scholarship for deserving Negro students.

Exploiting Racial Tensions

Nevertheless, the Birchers seek to exploit racial tensions, unrest and disorders for their own purposes. Forty-eight hours after the Watts riots in Los Angeles in the summer of 1965, Birch chapters were mobilized — via a directive to all area chapter leaders — for an intensive anti-civil rights propaganda drive to exploit the white reaction to the outburst of violence and disorder.

It is inevitable that, like the Communists, the Birchers will seek, in this way, to exploit racial tensions and outbursts of violence. During 1965, Birch propaganda had much to say about the Selma Civil Rights March — some of it indistinguishable from the outpourings of openly racist organizations in the Deep South.

In the June, 1965, issue of *American Opinion,* writer Jim Lucier described the Selma march as having been "organized by the International Conspiracy of Evil." An unsigned article in the July issue purported to describe what happened "when a horde of termites from all over the country, led by half-crazed ministers and professors, swarmed over the small town of Selma, Ala., in a typical demonstration of Communist activism."

It would be hard to finger such explosive "educational" prose as a direct cause of violence in the South but it is equally difficult to see in it any indication of an attempt to restore the racial harmony which Robert Welch, born and raised on a North Carolina farm, claims existed in the past.

Welch's Happy Vision

Welch has described such visions. In the June, 1965, *Bulletin,* he wrote of "that huge reservoir of good will between the races that was such a happy circumstance of American life only two decades ago." And in a recent television interview he saw that period (a time of Negro second-class citizenship and enforced Jim Crow vassalage) as having included "a very, very tiny amount of injustice."

Such may be the cornerstone of the racial attitudes the John Birch Society is building; the "happy circumstance" was one of segregation and inequality.

The quarrel of the Birch Society with the concept of Negro equality goes far deeper than mere questions of politics and methods, or even of the alleged Communist character of the civil rights movement itself.

● In *The Blue Book* of the Society, Welch decried democracy as "merely a deceptive phrase, a weapon of demagoguery, and a perennial fraud." In a footnote he added that democracy was "the worst of all forms of government."

● Jim Lucier, a frequent contributor to *American Opinion,* argued in the June, 1965, issue that (1) Voting is not one of the basic rights of a human being; (2) There is no direct relationship between voting and freedom; and (3) The doctrine of majority rule is alien to American political tradition and ideals.

● In the November, 1964, issue, National Council member Revilo P. Oliver, described by Welch as "quite possibly the world's greatest living scholar," wrote that it was a lie that the races are equal.

● In the February, 1965, issue, National Council member Tom Anderson wrote that "the right to discriminate is the right to choose and the right to choose is the essence of liberty."

Tainted Sources

Welch and those who wage war at his side are not always careful about the sources they cite to back up their contentions:

In the June, 1965, Birch *Bulletin,* for instance, Welch quoted "the long and prophetically accurate December, 1956 Special Report of the American Flag Committee." The American Flag Committee had predicted nine years earlier, he said, that 1965 was marked by the Communists as the target year for agitation for Negro voting rights. Welch devoted five full pages of the *Bulletin* to this report, and cited the American Flag Committee in five separate references.

The American Flag Committee was, in fact, a small-time propaganda outfit run by W. Henry MacFarland, Jr., of Philadelphia, an outspoken anti-Semite who toured the country some years ago with Gerald Smith, the anti-Jewish rabble-rouser. MacFarland cooperated with the late Conde McGinley, Jew-baiting publisher of *Common Sense,* and with the gutter-level, racist and anti-Semitic National Renaissance Party, headed by James Madole of New York, a minor pamphleteer and street corner agitator.

Welch's members had no way of knowing that two of the organizations founded by MacFarland before he created the American Flag Committee were included in the U. S. Attorney General's so-called list of subversive organizations. One was MacFarland's Nationalist Action League; the other, the Committee for Nationalist Action.

The July-August, 1965, issue of *American Opinion* gave source credit, in an evaluation of racial questions, to *The Councilor,* a blatantly racist and openly anti-Semitic publication edited in Shreveport, La., by Ned Touchstone. *The Councilor* is the organ of the White Citizens Councils of Louisiana.

What of the John Birch Society and the Ku Klux Klans, now waging guerrilla race warfare in the American South? Welch and Society Public Relations Director John Rousselot have made it clear that Klan members are not welcome in the John Birch Society.

However, take the case of Dr. John R. Andrew of Stone Mountain, Ga. Andrew was the leader of the Birch Society's Emory (Atlanta) chapter until he resigned the position early in 1965 to run for political office. He is still a member of the Society, and the Emory chapter still meets in his home. On August 23, 1965, Dr. Andrew addressed a rally of the Ku Klux Klan (United Klans of America) in Atlanta. He told the assembled Klansmen that he had been defeated in the special election for the reapportioned state legislature by the international banking conspiracy. Later, Andrew told a reporter for the Atlanta *Journal* that he was not actually a Klan member but would like to help the organization if he could.

Andrew was present on September 13, 1965, at the Henry Grady Hotel in Atlanta — as were Mr. and Mrs. George Birch (parents of John Birch) and other local Society luminaries — to hear a speech by former Major General Edwin A. Walker. During the question period, Walker, always proudly a Birch Society member, told a cheering audience:

"There will be a KKK in the USA longer than there will be an LBJ."

When, on August 10, 1965, at Long Beach, Calif., Walker told his hearers of the Red plot aimed at "you, the white race — just ninety miles from Florida," he was giving perhaps the ultimate expression to the politico-racial fears that have emerged as the wellspring of John Birch Society activity.

Purposes

The stated purpose of the Society's anti-civil rights campaign was set forth by Welch in a July, 1965, pamphlet entitled *A Stick of Dynamite*. The Society, he wrote, was not strong enough to fight a war, but it was strong enough to fight a battle and have a chance of success if it concentrated its forces on one front.

What are the true purposes of the Society's all-out attack on the civil rights movement?

● It is a convenient instrument for exploiting whatever white backlash exists in the nation as the result of the Negro thrust for equality.

● The propaganda campaign is a logical preliminary to Welch's plan for a Birch Society effort in 1966 to influence the Congressional elections.

● The campaign offers an opportunity for nationwide activity by Birchers, using TACT and other front groups, and for recruiting new members into the Society's ranks.

In short, like the Communists, the John Birch Society is seeking to exploit the nation's racial tensions for its own propaganda and recruitment purposes, and for its deeper political goals. And it is using the Communist technique of the front group as a propaganda and recruiting instrument.

15

3   *The Birch 'Line'*

The Society's extreme view of the civil rights struggle — that it is directed by an "International Communist Conspiracy" or, more mysteriously, by an "International Conspiracy of Evil"— represents only a portion of the standard Birch line on the origin and nature of the nation's problems.

Behind this theme stands a whole philosophy — the Conspiracy Theory of History — based on the belief that there exists an historic, unbroken, secret, and thoroughly committed succession of inter-related human beings dedicated with perverse monomania to evil purposes. "It is clear," to the Birch Society's Revilo P. Oliver (in *American Opinion,* December, 1964), "that there is in the human species some biological strain of either atavism or degeneracy that manifests itself in a hatred of mankind and a lust for evil for its own sake." The proponents of this hatred and lust are The Conspirators.

In the Birch view, the Conspiracy involves the very leadership of the United States Government for three decades and the present-day thrust of American policy at home and abroad.

A Communist America?

The Birch Society's latest evaluation of the United States (in the July-August "Scoreboard" issue of Welch's magazine) is that it is 60% to 80% under Communist influence and control. And the term "influence" must not be interpreted too softly, for the magazine's explanatory notes are more explicit:

16

"Americans can expect *only* defeat so long as they are commanded by their enemies."

In explaining their reasons for announcing an increase in the percentage of Communist control in the U. S. over 1964, the editors wrote:

"Although some believe that the bracket of 50% to 70% could be retained, there is substantial agreement that the percentage of control is now more than 60%, and no analysis supported a lower estimate."

And they added a built-in defense:

"It is not too much to say that the Conspiracy's greatest single asset in the whole world today is the fact that our score will seem utterly unbelievable and preposterous to so large a part of the American people."

And yet, from the same article: "Communist domination of many departments of the federal government is too obvious to require much comment."

Target: State Department

One particular government department was singled out for especially violent attack — the State Department. It was branded as "Communist headquarters in Washington ..." And the policies of that department were seen as clear signs of conspiracy. The editors recalled "a vigorous action against the Communists in Korea, which traitors in Washington quickly transformed into a very successful device for getting Americans killed, squandering American money, subjecting the United States to a humiliating defeat ..."

And they apply The Conspiracy Theory to more recent events, such as those in the Dominican Republic, where "the State Department is now busily installing another Communist base," or in Vietnam where the extent of Viet Cong penetration led correspondent Eric Butler (*American Opinion,* June, 1965) to write that "the only reasonable conclusion" was "that the situation was deliberately produced through treachery in Washington. . . . There has been no indication that American policymakers have any other intention ..."

The Enemies in Washington ...

We are, in the eyes of the Birch Society, commanded by

our enemies. Hence, say the editors of *American Opinion:*

"As for Vietnam, one thing is certain: No action really detrimental to the Communists is conceivable, or even *possible,* so long as Rusk, McNamara, and Katzenbach remain in power."

Robert Welch leveled the same accusation of treason at the top in an interview at Boston in August, 1964. "The Communists have absolutely no worry about bombs," he said, because "they control the men on both sides who would give the order to march — not the generals, but the politicians here and abroad."

The hunt for what Welch's magazine has referred to as "these secret forces" can lead, at worst, to the acceptance of awful imaginings as views of reality. Revilo P. Oliver, writing in the December, 1964, issue of *American Opinion,* said:

"In the mid-1930s ... there were reports that experimental stations in Asiatic Russia had pens of human women whom the research workers were trying to breed with male apes in the hope of producing a species better adapted to life under Socialism than human beings."

The same obsession with conspiracy leads, at best, to a divisive propaganda, creating fear and suspicion that belie claims of patriotism.

The Birch Society's charges of treason leveled against America's national leadership, undiminished since Welch's accusation that President Eisenhower was a Communist agent, expanded into a litany of wild indictments against President Johnson after the most recent Presidential election. In a melodramatic throwaway headlined "If you are one of the 27,000,000 then read this ..." the Society found not one, but rather 42,000,000 traitors, brainwashed by the Communist conspiracy:

"In November, 1964 forty-two million supporters of Lyndon Johnson voted for repeal of our Declaration of Independence ...

"voted for scrapping the United States Constitution entirely ...

"voted for encouragement and support by the Federal Government of racial agitators to instigate more riots ...

"voted for governmental steps and policies which will

gradually wipe out the value of all of their savings . . .

"Our forty-two million Johnson camp followers . . . voted to condone and accept the gradual destruction of all moral principles . . .

"Forty-two million Americans voted for communizing our nation . . ."

The Birch line on such institutions as the United Nations and the Supreme Court of the United States provides ample explanation of why "Get the US out of the UN" and "Impeach Earl Warren" have been made important national programs of the Society. The 1965 Scoreboard in *American Opinion* spoke of the international organization's peace-keeping machinery as the "Soviet-United Nations forces" and warned of "ruin wrought by the Bolsheviks . . . through their 'United Nations' front."

And it leveled at the Supreme Court an astounding charge:

"The efforts of the Warren Gang to produce a tidal wave of violence and crime are accomplishing their purpose."

The editors traced the efforts of the Chief Justice's "gang" throughout our juridical system, speaking of "the criminals whom the Conspiracy has slipped into lower courts, wherever it had an opportunity."

. . . And Those Elsewhere

The Birchers see the hand of the "conspiracy" in areas other than civil rights ("to instigate riots") and foreign policy ("getting Americans killed"). They view local police review boards as part of the secret plot; the income tax as a Marxist means of national suicide; the fluoridation of water as a means to produce a generation of "Mongolian idiots" (Oliver).

"Liberal intellectuals" are, in the view of Jim Lucier, in Welch's magazine, "inherently subversive."

Foreign aid, said the 1965 Scoreboard issue, "was naturally used to finance the Communist takeover of nation after nation [although] the ultimate purpose was to destroy our currency."

Birch Council member Tom Anderson, one of the most popular speakers before Birch audiences, speaks in the vernacular:

"We've got to take a stand against becoming a dictatorship. It's not the comrade I'm worried about, it's the liberal rat he is nesting with.

"If we have morality and courage we can destroy the diabolical conspiracy of communism. Every communist and every pro-communist ought to be arrested, deported and hung."

Robert Welch, taking a broad look at the national picture in a recent speech, declared:

"The United States is an insane asylum run by its worst patients."

And yet, the Birchers offer no hope for the "insane," for they view mental health programs as another Communist plot.

Sanity and Revilo P. Oliver

"The Communists," according to the Scoreboard editors, "in a very considerable number of states ... have induced the legislatures to enact 'mental health' laws to facilitate the incarceration of troublesome Americans." Americans first became aware of this, they added, on October 1, 1962, "when, in obedience to the specific demands of the Communist Party, a gang under the direction of Nicholas Katzenbach (now Attorney General of the United States) kidnapped General Edwin A. Walker in Oxford, Miss. ..."

Oliver took this line in an *American Opinion* article published in November, 1964, claiming that " 'mental health' prisons are being increasingly used for the kidnapping and mental, if not physical, murder of patriotic Americans."

It is Revilo Oliver of the Society's National Council who rides at the apogee of the Birch flight of mind. A classics professor at the University of Illinois, Oliver magnifies the terrors seen by the Right in triphammer prose, evoking from the members of the Birch Society greater acclaim than any other single spokesman. A tireless speaker on the Birch circuit, Oliver is also an official book reviewer for Welch's magazine — and as such, he recently gave a laudatory review to a blatantly anti-Semitic book, *World Revolution*.

The "Conspiracy" becomes Satanic in Revilo P. Oliver's eyes. It is he who claimed to see a strain of degeneracy in human beings which prompts them to form conspiracies of

20

hate. And now, he writes, "the power of government over us is being used, with a consistency and efficiency that must be intentional, to accelerate our deterioration and hasten our disappearance as a people by every means short of mass massacre . . ."

Oliver declared in a 1959 speech that Cuba is "an island largely populated by mongrels," and, in a January, 1965, *American Opinion* article, that Washington, D.C. is populated by "hordes of thieves, perverts, and traitors." He maintained, in November, 1964, that it is a lie that the races are equal, and a month later declared that "the United States is now engaged in an insane, but terribly effective, effort to destroy the American people and Western civilization by subsidizing, both at home and abroad, the breeding of the intellectually, physically, and morally unfit . . ."

In the November, 1964, *American Opinion,* Oliver contended that it is a lie that the Nazis killed six million Jews. (This, too, was an aspect of the secret plots for which Oliver has a practiced eye.)

In January, 1965, he wrote: "More than once, the directors of what calls itself the National Council of Churches have been caught in the very act of importing into the United States and escorting about the country identified agents of the Soviet Secret Police . . ." And in May, he accused the churches of spreading "confusion, fanaticism, and immorality."

Oliver on Kennedy

In discussing the work of the old Dies Committee (former Congressman Martin Dies, in *American Opinion,* has pointed with pride to his investigations of fascists), Oliver wrote in April, 1965, that the Dies Committee "also investigated a number of small American groups that the Communists called 'Fascist' because they were opposing in various ways Franklin D. Roosevelt's stealthy efforts to squander the lives and the money of the American people on a great Crusade to Save the Soviet."

It was Revilo P. Oliver who wrote the notorious "Marxmanship in Dallas," an *American Opinion* article charging that President Kennedy had been assassinated by Communist plotters because he was about to "turn American."

The man who pours out these fantasies is no mere Birch ally or hanger-on; he is a member of the John Birch Society's National Council and an associate editor of its magazine. Robert Welch has referred to him as "an authentic genius of the first water, *and quite possibly the world's greatest living scholar."*

And 1965's unsigned "Notes on the Scoreboard," in assessing the United States to be 60% to 80% in Communist control, drew this preliminary comment from editor Scott Stanley:

"We are especially grateful to Associate Editor Revilo P. Oliver for his hundreds of hours of examination, compilation, and microanalysis, which help to make the central editorial section of this issue one of the finest ever."

The Birch ideology holds that the United States today suffers from a cancerous disease called collectivism which stems in large measure from a huge plot. "Where there is no poverty," says Birch Council member Tom Anderson, "there is no freedom."

Human social progress is found to be degenerate, as well as conspiratorial, in the "microanalysis" of the 1965 *American Opinion* Scoreboard:

"Only when one looks closely does one see that the progress in *every* field ... is 'progress' toward barbarism, *designed* to weaken and destroy our moral instincts and our capacity for self-respect — *designed,* in short, to kill loyalty to the United States, respect for the white race, comprehension of Western civilization, and veneration of God. That simultaneous movement in a hundred supposedly unrelated segments of our national life cannot be mere coincidence."

The Conservative Awakening

After the appearance of the *American Opinion* 1965 Scoreboard issue, some American conservatives, including William F. Buckley, Jr., editor of *National Review* — blind for so long, and doggedly so — began to catch glimpses of the fact that many Birchers live in the same fantasy world as does Mr. Welch. Buckley and the others in his circle apparently realized — finally — that there is, indeed, a Radical Right in America, that Birch members agree with the

Birch leader, and that they are not merely misled conservatives, following a misguided leader.

Three of Buckley's syndicated columns in August, 1965, dealt with the Birch Society. In the first, on August 5, he enumerated the enormities contained in the Scoreboard issue of *American Opinion*. In the second, on August 17, he reprinted some of the indignant mail he had received from Birch members about his first column. In the third, on August 22, he finally reached the conclusion that there was no great ideological gap between Welch and those who march behind him in the Birch Society and who believe what Buckley called the Society's "paranoid and unpatriotic drivel."

Welch himself had already supplied the best answer about his followers years ago, in *The Blue Book*, when he declared:

"The men who join the John Birch Society during the next few months or few years are going to do so primarily because they believe in me and what I am doing and are willing to accept my leadership anyway."

More recently, Welch declared in a televised interview that "loyalty to an individual leader is harder to break down and tear to pieces than are a set of policy rules or principles . . ."

A Major Attack

Nevertheless, toward the end of 1965, the extremism of the Birch movement produced the beginnings of a significant split between the Birch radicals and the ultra-conservatives for whom Buckley is the most articulate spokesman.

The split, first signalled by Buckley's three syndicated columns, was then marked by a major attack in the form of a special six-part section in the October 19, 1965, issue of Buckley's *National Review,* and titled: "The John Birch Society and The Conservative Movement."

The essential thrust of the expose by the editors of *National Review* — Buckley, James Burnham and Frank S. Meyer — was that the Welchian concept of a United States in the grip of an internal Communist conspiracy holding 60 to 80% control over United States affairs and permeating the government itself, was a threat to the conservative movement; the more so because most, if not all, Birch members believe the Welchian mythology.

National Review last October quoted at length from Buckley's now-famous 1962 editorial in which he had criticized Welch, but not the Society members who follow Welch's leadership. *National Review* then pointed out:

"In the ensuing three years," three things had become clear: First, that Welch's views had not changed but on the contrary, had become "more virulent." Second, that there was no effective movement from within the Society "to contain Mr. Welch's utterances, or to remove him as the Society's leader." Third, that "Mr. Welch succeeds in influencing his membership to believe those surrealisms which he first ventilated in *The Politician;* and that as the membership comes to believe the Welch analysis, it ceases to be effectively anti-Communist."

Meyer's article, entitled "Principles and Heresies — The Birch Malady," concluded:

"The false analysis and conspiratorial mania of the John Birch Society has moved beyond diversion and waste of the devotion of its members to the mobilization of that devotion in ways directly anti-conservative and dangerous to the interests of the United States. It is no longer possible to consider the Society merely as moving towards legitimate objectives in a misguided way. However worthy the original motivations of those who have joined it and who apologize for it, it is time for them to recognize that the John Birch Society is rapidly losing whatever it had in common with patriotism or conservatism — and to do so before their own minds become warped by adherence to its unrolling psychosis of conspiracy."

Birchers and Vietnam

The article by James Burnham emphasized that on Vietnam, the Birch Society was "lined up with its supposedly diametric opposite, the Left, in support of Getting Out, not Standing Firm." Burnham said that the Birch stand on Vietnam, which found it on the same side as the Radical Left, stemmed from the Birch belief that for all intents and purposes today, the United States is a Communist nation and has a Communist government. Burnham concluded:

"Responsible conservatives have long tried to believe that the JBS, though 'misguided,' was 'going in the same direction' and therefore an 'ally.' Certainly this is the case with many, perhaps even most, individual JBS members. But unfortunately, under the years of brainwashing and organizational control by Robert Welch, the Society as a collective body has taken off in directions where no conservative can prudently venture, and has become a suitable ally only for confusion and sterility. Its stand on Vietnam confirms, not for the first time, that any American who seriously wants to contribute to his country's security and well-being and to oppose Communism will have to stay clear of the JBS."

In demolishing the over-simplifications of the Welchian and Birchite "Conspiratorial" view of history and events, and noting that "human reality is ignored . . . in the outlook of the John Birch Society," Meyer paused to deal with the Birch line that the civil rights movement in America is part of a Communist plot. He wrote:

"The sources of the civil rights movement are manifold. Certain just, if limited, grievances of the Negro people have been magnified, and have been extended to a challenge of our whole constitutional structure, primarily as a result of the operation of Liberal ideology. It is true that here (as everywhere it profits them) Communist groups are active, seeking to take advantage of the turmoil, and are sometimes successful in penetrating sections of the leadership of the movement. But the movement is not a Communist movement, as the John Birch Society implies with every device of rhetoric, with pictures, with innuendo, and often with straight-forward statement. There is, of course, much in the civil rights movement which conservatives should oppose; but when it is attacked in the Birch manner, on the basis of an obsessed insistence on conspiracy ('it's all a Communist plot'), sober opposition is discredited and great positive harm done the conservative cause."

4   *The JBS and Anti-Semitism*

In 1965, Welch gave a three-day seminar for a small group at a private home in the Midwest. His whole presentation was recorded and the 22-hour monologue was then edited down to 18 hours and issued by the Society as "One Dozen Trumpets" — twelve record albums of four sides each. Price: $50.

At one point in his marathon seminar, Welch touched on the subject of anti-Semitism. He said in part:

"Anti-Semitism has been the most powerful weapon the Communists have had at different times. In my opinion — I think you could prove it — anti-Semitism was created by the Communists for them to be able to use both sides. There was some hatred or dislike for Jews still left in Europe in the latter part of the 19th Century but not much. In America, practically none.

". . . the whole anti-Semitic thing had disappeared in the United States, as it had largely in Europe, 'til the Communists brought it back. They began to bring it back in the 1890s very strong.

"I have no slightest doubt that 'The Protocols of the Elders of Zion,' which has been used so extensively and disastrously to create trouble, was written either by Lenin or for Lenin deliberately to serve their purposes in many ways.

"There is no doubt, in my opinion, that it was a Communist who twisted Henry Ford, Sr., into making such a dope of himself in his book and so forth, and creating situations that would make him so angry and cause him to do these things. And the Communists used that. . . .

"In my opinion — and I don't know whether I'll leave this in this tape or not — maybe not — because I want to write a book about it — but the greatest creator of anti-Semitism in the United States for the last generation has been, of course, the Anti-Defamation League. Done more to create anti-Semitism, under the guise of stopping it and preventing it, than all other organizations put together. But what's more important — in my opinion — that's what it was founded for; that was its purpose — was to create anti-Semitism. Just as so many other things that the Communists have had a hand in behind the scenes are created for the exact opposite of what they appear to be created for. And the ADL has done an incredibly good job of creating anti-Semitism. . . .

"Thus a first of the great splits. Communists use both sides of it. We have members resign every week because we won't come out and fight the Jews. 'You must know that it's all the Jews — the whole conspiracy is Jewish — and of course Welch knows it, too, but he hasn't got the courage and he hasn't got the guts and he won't do it so why bother with the John Birch Society. Let's come on boys and fight the real enemy.'

"We have them resigning every week on that basis 'cause we won't fight the Jews and on the other side we're being smeared every week by at least two or three speeches by ADL on the grounds that we are anti-Semitic. Because it's Communists on both sides. Not that our members are Communists — they're being misled by Communists. They're playing both sides of the street as they do all streets, everywhere, all the time. Just as in Germany they created Hitler — the evidence is that he didn't know it — but they did — they created the whole Nazi Party and they drugged Hitler and the Nazi Party — which was not part of the original Hitler plan at all — into persecution of the Jews. There's no doubt that was planned and put into effect in Germany by Stalin 'cause it served their purposes there."

27

'Let's Suppose'...

In seeking to warn his members against anti-Semitism — which he has done repeatedly — Welch expanded on the whole theme in the November, 1965, *Bulletin:*

"Let's suppose you happen to believe, for instance, that the Anti-Defamation League, always under the guise of protecting the Jews from anti-Semitism — and certainly with that intention on the part of many of its leaders — has actually done more to cause and promote anti-Semitism than any other group or force in America. Suppose you even go further — as do some of my Jewish friends — and believe that the ADL was originally designed by Communists for that very purpose . . . then why on earth help them, and the Communists behind them, to carry out this nefarious scheme, by yourself reacting in exactly the way the Communists have planned and wanted?"

Welch also wrote in the same *Bulletin:*

". . . there came a period of some forty years when an abnormal percentage of the visible leadership of the Communist Conspiracy was of Jewish ancestry. . . . And these traitors to their race — as well as to all mankind — worked and schemed and plotted to have themselves hated, *not as Communists, but as Jews.*"

That Welch could imagine so fiendish a conspiracy is hardly surprising after one has read the first sentence quoted just above — an echo of the oldest anti-Semitic canards.

A JBS Problem

Welch has, in recent years, written several pieces that could be described as *anti-* anti-Semitic, manifestly in an effort to keep his organization free of anti-Jewish taint. But the Society has had a chronic problem with the instigators of religious hate it seems to attract and whom Welch brands as Communist *agents provocateurs.* And the Society has been less than successful in dealing with the problem.

The Society's trouble with anti-Semites is illustrated by the cases of Californians Richard Cotten and James Oviatt. Cotten, a radio propagandist who preaches that Communism was financed by "those people" in New York and that the U. S. State Department is run by Jews, has gathered adherents from among Birch Society members in the Far West — to whom he has recommended the publications of such hate mongers as Gerald Smith, Don Bell and Conde McGinley. He thus became a major cause of controversy and dissension within Welch's organization. The trouble became so acute by the spring of 1965 that Welch sent to every chapter leader in the United States a special, printed memorandum warning Birchers away from Cotten and his teachings. It was also Cotten's fondness for armed "anti-Communism" (such as that of the Minutemen) and for a particular Korean prophet Welch considered pro-Red, besides Cotten's blatant anti-Semitism, that aroused Welch's ire.

James Oviatt, a Los Angeles haberdasher who had been a member of the Society, was a patron of Wesley Swift, a notorious anti-Semite. Oviatt mailed to his store's clients packets of hate literature including material based on the classic fraud of anti-Semitica, "The Protocols of the Learned Elders of Zion." Oviatt was dropped by Welch from membership after the Anti-Defamation League made his activities public. In August, 1965, William F. Buckley, Jr., published a letter he had received from Oviatt after a previous Buckley blast against Welch and his Society's extremism. Oviatt wrote:

"I am just wondering what Zionist Jew wrote this article? Could it have been Lippmann, or Goldberg, or even Abe — Johnson's attorney? . . . I have known Bob Welch for over 15 years. I think he told the truth about Eisenhower."

At about the time of its expose of Oviatt, the ADL published an analysis of the anti-Semitism in articles written for Welch's magazine by Westbrook Pegler. Welch wrote the League: "We were already becoming unhappy ourselves with some of the attitudes in Mr. Pegler's writings."

In the meantime, *American Opinion* had dropped Pegler who went on to grace the platform of Gerald Smith. Late in 1965, he began writing a column for *The Councilor,* the racist, anti-Semitic organ of the Louisiana White Citizens Councils. It is worthy of note, however, that while Welch dropped Oviatt and Pegler, a Boston woman who has made financial contributions to Smith's anti-Jewish "Christian

Nationalist Crusade," Olive Simes, is still listed as a stockholder in *American Opinion* magazine.

The Anti-Semitic Background

The appearance of such persons as Olive Simes and Richard Cotten in the Birch apparatus are not isolated incidents — nor are they especially surprising. Welch and his Society have a lack of alertness — a kind of blind spot — about the activities in which such people have been engaged, even when such activities have been carefully made a matter of public knowledge.

As early as 1952, Welch cited a pamphlet by Joseph Kamp as source material for his book, *May God Forgive Us*. (Kamp is a long-time extremist pamphleteer whose writings have been filled with ill-concealed anti-Semitic innuendo.) Later, Welch paid Kamp $100 to check the manuscript of his 1954 book, *The Life of John Birch*. Still later, sections of Welch's infamous book on Eisenhower, *The Politician,* appeared to have been taken almost verbatim from the March 15, 1952, issue of Kamp's *Headlines*. (Welch later wrote he had not been aware that many considered Kamp to be an extremist pamphleteer and declared he would never allow the Birch Society to become a haven for anti-Semites so long as he was at its helm).

In *The Politician,* Lucille Miller of Bethel, Vt., was described by Welch as "a patriotic but not too cautious Vermont woman." Actually, she was a blatant anti-Semite, and had been so identified quite publicly.

Still another authority cited by Welch in his "Black Book" was Merwin Hart, who had been one of America's most prolific voices of anti-Semitism through almost three decades.

Hart, who died in 1962, had been active in Coughlinite and isolationist causes during the pre-World War II days. His association with Robert Welch first came to public view in 1959, when he was listed on the advisory board of the first Birch Society front group, the "Committee Against Summit Entanglements." Later, Hart appeared in the Birch apparatus as a Society chapter leader. At least two supporters of Hart's National Economic Council have served as members of the National Council of the Birch Society.

In spite of Welch's periodic admonitions, the tendency of

the John Birch Society to attract anti-Semites has persisted, and plagues the organization. Welch again recognized the problem when, in 1963, he issued a pamphlet called *The Neutralizers,* criticizing and warning against those who "neutralized" the Birch Society's program with fits of irrelevant anti-Semitism or with "tangentitis" (fanatical support for Right Wing causes other than those canonized by the Society itself).

The pamphlet assailed some of the fundamental tenets of the Jew-haters and singled out bigot Wesley Swift and the "British-Israel" cult of Anglo-Saxon racism for criticism. It did not mention Merwin Hart or Joe Kamp. What is perhaps most significant in *The Neutralizers* is the fact that it had to be written at all and that Welch found it necessary to devote 16 pages to the task of proving to the membership of his Society that Communism is *not* a Jewish conspiracy.

The Anti-Semitic Foreground

The attraction of anti-Semites to the John Birch Society has not gone un-noticed. As pointed out earlier, the Society made wide and exhaustive use of the report of the first investigation of the Society by California's Senate Fact-Finding Sub-Committee on Un-American Activities in 1963, although understandably saying little or nothing about a more recent report by the same body in June, 1965. The 1965 report found "an influx of emotionally unstable people" into the Society and a "dangerous increase of anti-Semitism among a minority of membership."

Rousselot was quoted at that time by the Associated Press as explaining: "We have been concerned with the problem of anti-Semitic infiltrators." (By thus labeling anti-Semites as outside "infiltrators," he apparently sought to avoid what is actually an inherent problem of the Society and to dodge its implications.) Rousselot added: "We have dealt very decisively with the problem."

On the other hand, in the *Bulletin* for November, 1965, Welch suggests that the ADL stirs up the problem "by unjustly accusing people of anti-Semitism."

Recent events and activities make it possible to judge whether "unjust" accusations are involved, and to evaluate just how "decisively" Robert Welch has dealt with the problem of keeping the Birch Society free of anti-Semitic taint. These specifics represent a sampling of the available evidence:

Item: "The Patriot's Book Shelf and American Opinion Library" in San Bernardino, Calif., has had available the material of several anti-Semitic propagandists — Marilyn Allen, Richard Cotten, Myron Fagan, Kenneth Goff and Wickliffe Vennard.

Item: The same store has stocked "De Gaulle — Rothschild's Pawn," published by the Christian Educational Association, of Union, N. J. (which also publishes the viciously anti-Jewish *Common Sense*). The pamphlet offered in the San Bernardino store — which has the official recommendation of the Society's West Coast headquarters as a Birch book outlet — finds that "officials appointed by De Gaulle from 1940 to date have included at least TWENTY- FOUR JEWS, NINE SOCIALISTS, SEVEN COMMUNISTS, FIVE FRIENDS OF ISRAEL, and FOUR MARRIED TO JEWESSES!" (Capitals and exclamation in the original).

Item: The American Opinion Bookstore in Mobile, Ala., has distributed a flyer advertising *The Other Side of the Coin,* by Alfred Lilienthal. The flyer quotes a passage from the book explaining that anti-Semitism is not the product of anti-Semites, but rather "the conspiracy of the rabbinate, Jewish nationalists and other leaders of organized Jewry. . . ."

Item: The American Opinion Library in Stratford, Conn., has sold a booklet entitled *Parents Are Puppets of the P-TA,* published by the right-wing Tarrant County Public Affairs Forum in Fort Worth, Texas. The booklet bore a sticker stating: "Order from Christian Educational Assn., Union, New Jersey" — the publisher, as noted, of the notoriously anti-Semitic periodical *Common Sense* and a purveyor of various anti-Jewish reprints. An examination of a number of these booklets available at the Stratford Birch store showed that many bore the same sticker. The booklet itself contained a sly reference to Dr. Leo Pasvolsky, active in the formation of the United Nations, as "a Russian-born Zionist who was Assistant U.S. Secretary of State from 1936-1946."

Item: The American Opinion Bookstore in Seattle,

Wash., has sold an "anti-Communist" booklet by Kenneth Goff, an ex-lieutenant of Gerald Smith's, and a notorious anti-Semite for almost 20 years.

Item: Poor Richard's Book Shop of Hamilton, Mont., (formerly of Los Angeles), whose proprietor has been identified as a Birch member, has openly advertised anti-Semitic and racist books in its catalogue, and (less openly, from under its own counter) has sold *Pawns in the Game,* a rehash of the *Protocols of the Elders of Zion.*

Item: The American Opinion Library of Syracuse (N.Y.), Inc., one of the East's major suppliers for Birch Society bookstores (it wholesales to other bookstores), has sold Nesta H. Webster's *World Revolution — The Plot Against Civilization,* a book originally published in England forty-four years ago, which attempts to portray a conspiratorial Jewish power lurking behind Communism. The author quotes copiously from what she calls "the amazing *Protocols of the Elders of Zion.*"

Item: Mrs. Webster's malicious book has also been sold in the Birchers' bookstores in Freeport, L. I. (N.Y.) ; Albany, Calif., and Stamford, Conn. The Stamford store, moreover, has displayed pamphlets by Joseph Kamp and copies of the *Economic Council Letter.*

Item: Mrs. Webster's book was reviewed very favorably by Revilo P. Oliver in the January, 1965, issue of *American Opinion.* Oliver called the anti-Semitic book "simply indispensable" to students of the "conspiracy." He also found its author, who had been an admirer of fascism, to be "one of the most gracious and charming of Englishwomen." Oliver, who likes to remind his readers that Jack Ruby's name once had been Rubenstein, was once a featured speaker at a convention of the "Soldiers of the Cross," the organization headed by Kenneth Goff, the notorious anti-Semite.

Item: A second, and equally anti-Semitic book by Mrs. Webster, entitled *Secret Societies and Subversive Movements,* was sold in the Albany, Calif., American Opinion Library.

(Mrs. Webster's book on world revolution was reprinted by the Owen Publishing Co., Waco, Texas, and was advertised in *American Opinion* magazine of January, 1965, — the same issue in which Oliver praised it in his review.

Mrs. Webster's book on secret societies was reprinted by Omni Publications, Hawthorne, Calif., which advertised it in the February, 1965, issue of the Birch periodical. Owen Publishing Co. is owned by Homer L. Owen, formerly editor of "The Fighting American" in which he reprinted material from anti-Semitic sources during 1960 and 1961.)

Item: A pamphlet written by Joseph Kamp, attacking Jewish leaders, was one of the pieces offered for sale at the 1965 Rally for God, Family, and Country (Boston, July 4) — a rally run by several members of the Birch Society headquarters staff and traditionally including a testimonial dinner to Robert Welch.

Item: Earlier in 1965, a letter was circulated in Farmland, Ind., attacking the Anti-Defamation League as "a secret police . . . (an) atom-powered Communist front." The description was admittedly quoted from a leaflet by a notorious anti-Jewish propagandist of the 1950s — Major Robert H. Williams. The letter was signed, "Farmland Members of the John Birch Society."

Item: Benjamin Freedman, an apostate Jew, pro-Arab and anti-Zionist propagandist, financial backer of anti-Semites, addressed a series of three very secret meetings arranged on their own by several Birch members on Long Island (N.Y.) early in 1965. Invitation to the three sessions of anti-Jewish invective was by word of mouth only, and extended only to Birchers and their close friends.

A Voice Near the Top

Birch Society officials may insist that even such anti-Semitic weeds as these grow only on the lower fringes of their domain, where they cannot easily be seen and plucked out — ignoring the supposed tight control and efficiency of their monolithic system, and excusing the blindness and ineffectiveness that has characterized their handling of the problem over the whole of the Society's seven years.

Such a defense by Society officers is, however, irrelevant in view of at least one manifestation of its know-nothing posture: a man recognized for over a quarter of a century as one of Australia's leading anti-Semites is now a regular correspondent of the John Birch Society's magazine — and this position is far from the lower fringes of the apparatus.

"Eric D. Butler," says his biographical sketch in *American Opinion,* "is National Director of The League of Rights, Australia's most significant anti-Communist organization." The adjective *significant* has been used elsewhere, however, to describe the League of Rights as "the most significant organized anti-Semitic group" in that country.

Eric Butler founded the League of Rights and has edited its publication, the *New Times,* in which he himself wrote, on September 26, 1947:

> "Ever since their active participation in the crucifixion of Christ, the Jewish leaders have worked ceaselessly to undermine and destroy the Christian faith. They have always believed and still believe in the Chosen Race idea; that the Jewish leaders are destined to rule the world."

Anti-Jewish Book

In that same year, Butler wrote his own version of the notorious *Protocols,* a 166-page book entitled, *The International Jew — The Truth About the Protocols of Zion.* A spokesman for the Catholic archdiocese of Sydney called Butler's work "a childish exhibition of anti-Semitism at its worst . . . a disgraceful and mischievous production which is calculated to do harm to its readers . . ."

But the book won the praise of the hate press in the United States. It was cheered and quoted, for example, by bigots Elizabeth Dilling and Lyrl Van Hyning in their hate publications.

Eric Butler's views showed no change through the years. In the September 12, 1958 issue of the *New Times,* the following appeared:

> "What is meant by the word gentleman does not exist among Jews. The genuine Jew fails in this innate good breeding . . ."

In 1960, Butler wrote a pamphlet in which he declared:

> ". . . the constant repetition of the statement that the Germans murdered six million Jews is without doubt one of the most frightening examples of the successful use of the big lie technique . . . to exaggerate the number of Jews murdered in order to make it easier for the Political

35

Zionists to try and justify their own murderous and totalitarian policies . . ."

A *New Times* editorial on June 16, 1962, spoke of "the vital role played by Jews in the Communist espionage systems," and then warned:

"People who attempt to discuss national and international politics as if this Jewish power does not exist, are either very naive or they are very frightened."

Butler's Book Shop

While he published such views, Butler's own Heritage Bookshop sold a variety of anti-Jewish standards, including Col. John O. Beaty's *The Iron Curtain Over America,* which makes exhaustive use of the *Protocols,* Benjamin Freedman's *Facts Are Facts,* and Louis Marschalko's *The World Conquerors.*

Eric Butler came to the United States in January, 1964, and on the 19th of that month, addressed a meeting of the "Citizens' Congressional Committee" in Los Angeles. The meeting was held under the chairmanship of Gerald Smith.

A few months later, "Christian Youth Against Communism," a front group of Gerald Smith's organization, published Butler's speech as a 30-page pamphlet.

Later that spring, Butler made a tour of Canadian cities under the sponsorship of Ron Gostick, publisher of the anti-Semitic *Canadian Intelligence Service* and long an admirer of Butler. At about the same time, Butler's latest booklet, *The Red Pattern of World Conquest,* appeared on the American scene. Butler briefly injected (on page 65) his usual anti-Jewish thinking:

"The reasons why so many Jews have been prepared to act as espionage agents are understandable, but we need not go into this highly emotional subject in this story . . ."

In the spring of 1965 some disturbing anonymous mailings began to emanate from the State of Washington and from British Columbia, containing reprints of some 32 pages of Butler's *The International Jew.* At the bottom of the final page, the following note appeared:

"In printing this work on behalf of Mr. E. D. Butler, the printers, R. M. Osborne Limited, of 95 Currie Street,

Adelaide, desire it to be known that the views expressed therein are those of the author and do not necessarily represent their views."

'Far East Correspondent'

It was at about the same time — April, 1965 — that Eric Butler's first article in *American Opinion* appeared. Others have been published regularly since then, and the Birch Society publication describes Butler as its "regular Far East correspondent."

In the 1965 Scoreboard issue — wherein "Communist" influence in each nation of the world is judged annually — Butler was assigned, ironically, to cover the area of Arab-Israel tensions. On Israel he reported: "This country's politics must be assessed against its pro-Communist background." This view may, perhaps, be "assessed" against the author's own background.

In October, 1965, a report was made at a synod of the Australian Anglican Church by its Vicar, the Rev. D. J. Pope, alleging that an anti-Semitic group was engaged in secret infiltration of the churches. He charged that the group was spreading the lie "that the Jews are trying to seize control of the world," and that it was "reviving old techniques used against the Jews." The Vicar identified the infiltrating group as the "League of Rights" — the organization founded and directed by Robert Welch's own Far East "expert."

5   *Program and Activities*

The peculiar John Birch view of reality — the United States seen as 60-80% Communist-controlled, of 19th Century America as some sort of idyllic pinnacle of civilization, and most subsequent American history as the disastrous result of diabolical conspiracies — has attracted significant numbers of Right Wing radicals. It has produced, necessarily, a program to satisfy needs that have obviously led to successful organization. Officially, action is limited to the dissemination of a barrage of propaganda — books, flyers, tapes, films, rally speeches, petitions, and bumper stickers — to the infiltration of various civic, political, church, and school organizations, to the formation of front committees and to the writing of letters. But often action has taken more subtle and disturbing forms under the traditional Birch mantle of secrecy and the Welch dictum that justifies the use at times of "mean and dirty" tactics.

The National Activities

Some analysts have suggested that the Society's national program amounts to little more than the hard recruiting of new members — that all else is propaganda developed for recruitment purposes. In any event, the Society's basic biases have spawned certain causes and crusades which form the framework of its national effort. To this framework are hung the local front groups, the flood of pseudo-educational materials disseminated through a network of bookstores, and the loyalties of the members themselves.

38

The Society's early scattered shots at enemies far and wide have been gradually narrowed down to selected targets described in the Standard Agenda in the September, 1963, *Bulletin*. It is into this agenda, with only slight variations, that the national program has been jelled:

I. Recruiting . . .
II. The Movement to Impeach Warren . . .
III. The United Nations — Get US Out . . .
IV. Civil Rights . . .
V. The Liberty Amendment . . .
(abolish income tax)
VI. Support Your Local Police . . .
VII. American Opinion . . .
VIII. American Opinion Libraries . . .
IX. American Opinion Speakers Bureau . . .
X. Conduct Study Clubs . . .
XI. The Review of the News . . .
XII. Your Own Reading . . .

The *Bulletin* urges support for some of the above items (e.g., Liberty Amendment) and damnation for others (e.g., Civil Rights). A series of Temporary Projects often follows — a torrent of letters to some unsuspecting senator, perhaps, or greeting cards to a Welch hero.

The Attack on the UN

"There are more Communists in the United Nations building in New York than there are in the Kremlin." So wrote Robert Welch in the Society's *Bulletin* for May, 1965. As Public Relations Director Rousselot states it:

"The UN was originally designed and planned by key Communist sympathizers, and today the organization is controlled and administered by the Communists."

When Rousselot made this charge in a speech at the Birch-dominated 1965 Rally for God and Country in Boston, G. Edward Griffin, a Society official from California, turned to the Eastern Public Relations Director, Tom Davis, and commented: "He's read my book."

Griffin's book, *The Fearful Master,* has recently been the Birch Society's chief weapon in the propaganda assault against the United Nations.

The author, comparing Americans to suicidal lemmings, writes that in supporting the United Nations, the United States "abandoned the secure ground of national strength and independence to leap into the boiling waters of internationalism." He sees the UN itself as a nest of spies and Communist murderers; says that loyalty to the UN is being designed to supplant loyalty to the United States, and that the loyalty eventually demanded will be to world Communism. These facts, he concludes, are all hidden from the American people because the UN, like all enemies of the Birch Society, is secret and conspiratorial.

Other anti-UN materials of the Society include postcards (a picture of the UN building labeled "The House That Hiss Built"), stickers of various sizes with the slogan "The UN — Get US Out" which are available for envelopes or auto bumpers, a special $2 packet of propaganda which includes the Griffin book and a purported expose of the World Health Organization by J. B. Matthews.

In Michigan, a group of Birchers added a wrinkle of their own when they flew over the stadium at the 1964 Michigan-Minnesota football game in a helicopter dragging a 50-foot "Get US Out" trailer.

Mass Letter Writing

The Society's national anti-UN campaign has included several massive letter-writing efforts. In his November, 1964, *Bulletin,* Welch requested all Birch members to bombard Mrs. Norman Chandler, Walt Disney, and other directors of the new Los Angeles Music Center with mail protesting a decision to fly the UN flag over the project. For whatever reason, the flag did not fly, and Welch crowed of a victory.

In 1964, the John Birch Society declared war on the Xerox Corporation — after the company had announced its sponsorship of a projected series of television specials on the United Nations. Robert Welch immediately urged his members to send "a veritable flood" of letters to the corporation.

Xerox received 29,500 pieces of adverse mail even before the first broadcast reached the screen. A tabulation revealed that the 29,500 letters had been sent by only 6,000 individuals! During the next six months, in which Welch wrote several reminders, the company received another 15,700 letters, analyzed as having come from only 5,500 individuals. (During the same period Xerox received 4,400 pro-UN letters from about 4,400 individuals.)

The Movement to Impeach Earl Warren

Visitors to the Indianapolis Speedway on Memorial Day, 1965, could not miss the huge outdoor billboard opposite the entrance. It advised:

"Save Our Republic. Impeach Earl Warren!"

The mammoth advertising space had been contracted by a local group calling itself the "Committee for Outdoor Advertising to Save Our Republic." A similar sign greeted the civil rights marchers just outside the city of Selma, Ala., during their famous march early in 1965. There, the billboard was signed "The John Birch Society." There are hundreds of "Impeach Earl Warren" billboards on streets, roads and highways all across the country. The campaign is a Birch project.

The Birchers' appeal in the Selma area was, intentionally or not, to certain obvious emotions. But the official purposes of their now-famous "Movement to Impeach Earl Warren" are much broader. Welch wrote in the March, 1965, *Bulletin* that the proposal to impeach the Chief Justice of the United States was intended "to make men behave, not to give them more laws to distort and ignore. And the way to make the Justices on the present Supreme Court behave is to impeach the ringleader in their judicial crimes . . ."

In May, Welch assessed the effort: "If and when we can make enough good citizens informed enough and aroused enough to force the impeachment of Warren, we shall have won a battle of tremendous importance in the total war." In short, the Society wants to persuade "good citizens" that the court of ultimate appeal in this country today is besmirched by terrible treason. The idea was expressed in an unsigned article in the July-August, 1965, issue of *American Opinion:*

"The theory that the Warren Court is working for a domestic, as distinct from foreign, dictatorship becomes less tenable every day."

To advance the idea of such infamy in high places the

41

Birch Society sells a Warren Impeachment Packet — a $2.45 bundle of propaganda for $1, which includes the Robert Welch leaflet, *Republics and Democracies* (condemning democracy), and two pamphlets by Mississippi's Senator James O. Eastland (one entitled *Is the Supreme Court Pro-Communist?*).

Welch continually urges circulation of the packet, of a series of *Dan Smoot Reports* on the same subject, and of a one-page compendium entitled *Why Warren Should Be Impeached* — all explanations of "the role played by Earl Warren in the destruction of our republic." The large billboard posters displayed at Selma and elsewhere across the land are available through Society headquarters at $20.

An Aborted Plan

A group of avid Birchers in the New York metropolitan area, encouraged by the Society's huge local growth during the election campaign, began secretly to plan an Impeach Warren saturation drive in the spring of 1965. It was to burst upon the tri-state area of New York, New Jersey, and Connecticut like an unexpected comet on April 1 — with airplane trailers and motor cavalcades, spot advertising, sound trucks, rallies, and thousands of posters and billboards. But Belmont was never consulted on the plan. This was, in Welch's words, "due to the worst failure, or lapse, of communication within our staff organization itself, in the history of the Society." The result was the sacking of the local coordinator and a wrist-slapping for the New York Birchers who were guilty of straying from the proper authority within the Society monolith. Welch softened the blow by stating that most of their plans and materials could be "used to full advantage at a later date."

In the June, 1965, Birch *Bulletin*, Welch aimed the impeachment campaign in a frankly political direction. He reported the Society's "announced intention of making the question of Warren's impeachment a very important criterion by which to judge Congressional candidates in the Summer of 1966." Many on the American Right have been disturbed by Welch's goal of impeachment for the Chief Justice of the United States. They ask, why impeachment, instead of remedial legislation proposed by some ultra-conservatives?

Welch's answer: it is "simply that not enough people understand, or will get excited about, amendments to limit the appellate jurisdiction of the Supreme Court. . . . While anybody and everybody can understand, and quickly acquire very strong feelings about, the impeachment of Earl Warren."

The Community Level

The influence of the John Birch Society — and of the Radical Right in general — is often most effective, most easily seen, and most keenly felt at the grass-roots level of American life. It is in the community that their political plans and their hopes to reverse the direction of American life and government — and even of world affairs — must inevitably begin. It is at the local level — in hundreds of cities, suburbs, towns and hamlets — that the 5,000 Birch chapters and the 80,000 or so Birch members have been feverishly toiling in recent years.

Robert Welch fully understands the importance of local community groups, civic organizations and voluntary committees in American life. He knows full well that the Birchers must penetrate and influence these vital sinews of American life if the Society is to achieve the counter-thrust it seeks at the national level — to repeal the last thirty years of American political, social and economic history since 1933.

The vital need for effective strength at the local level is obvious:

● Infiltration and the capture of positions of influence are more easily accomplished, and ultimately more effective, at the local level. The position of public librarian in the town of Boxford, Mass., for example, was held by a Birch member who had done public recruiting and organizing work for the Society. She lost her job after using it to promote the distribution of Birch literature through the library.

● The apathy of moderates is more in evidence, and offers more potent an opportunity for an extremist minority, at the local level. Turnouts for community or school board

43

elections, for example, are notoriously low almost everywhere.

● There is a greater emotional pull on issues that "hit home" — particularly when the emotions can be buttressed with a manufactured fear, or where neighborhoods are split in bitterness.

● Greater political pressure, concentrated and personal, can be brought to bear on local, county and state officials, and on local businessmen.

● Pressures can be tightly organized, and it is easy to mount saturation propaganda drives reaching great percentages of the local population.

In the Washington, D.C.-Maryland area, where substantial Birch Society growth has recently taken place, activity is energetic and well-financed. A heavy volume of Birchite propaganda is distributed through six local book outlets. The membership has influential friends at state and county legislative levels. In the Baltimore area, Birchers and their allies were instrumental in campaigns to kill an urban renewal program and various poverty program projects. In several Maryland counties they have been able to distribute Society materials to teachers in the schools. This is typical of Birch effectiveness on the local community level.

'Front' Groups

A major Birch activity in communities from coast to coast has been the establishment of front groups — often used as cloaks of respectability or anonymity — through which the national programs of the Society can be adapted to the local scene and new members lured into cooperation first and recruitment later. Very often these are committees named as being in "support of the police," or of "law and order," or of "God in our schools." Many have been called the "Committee to get the US Out of the UN"— although under the Birch drive for respectability, a New England group of that name became the "Committee to Promote Understanding of the United Nations." There are, likewise, many "Committees to Impeach Earl Warren"— but one in California's San Gabriel Valley has become the "Committee for Judicial Re-Education."

The "Southeastern Massachusetts Educational Committee" apparently has but one educational activity — it shows the new Birch Society recruiting film in and around the city of Taunton.

In newspaper advertisements, the Wakefield (Mass.) Forum not long ago announced a lecture series under its sponsorship at the Wakefield Memorial High School. The Forum did not identify itself as a Birch operation. But a local citizen, whose only Far Right link had been his registration on July 4, 1965, at Boston's "Rally for God and Country" (which itself had officially denied Birch Society affiliation), received a mailing from the Society's national headquarters in September. It included a handful of Birch literature, an application for tickets to the Wakefield Forum, and a map showing routes to the Wakefield High School.

The American Opinion Forum of Long Island (N.Y.), which also sponsored a series of "conservative" speakers, was more obvious. Its usherettes wore uniforms emblazoned with a gold-embroidered "JBS."

The purpose of such Committees and Forums is to expose the public to Birch ideology with the aim of recruitment — usually under the cloak of some righteous-sounding cause. The chairman of Connecticut's "Christian Committee for Prayers in Schools," for example, is the John Birch Society's paid state coordinator.

By infiltrating community organizations — school, civic, and church groups — and by harassing those it cannot dominate, or those of an opposing viewpoint (such as those fostering Civil Rights, civil liberties or the UN), the local Birch apparatus seeks to gain that measure of grass-roots control that is the necessary base of power.

Attempted Takeovers

When a number of residents in Mount Prospect, Ill., called a preliminary meeting for the formation of a human relations council, the local Birch chapter leader (Chapter QRKJ) alerted all Society members in the area to the potential danger of "left-wingers." The Birchers showed up in strength at an organizational meeting of the new anti-bias group, packing its membership. They managed to have their own people elected to office — some of whom had opposed formation of the council in the first place — and appointed

45

to draft the proposed by-laws. They made it clear they wanted the organization to take a strong stand against race-mixing, ("mongrelizing"), to watch out for Communists, and perhaps to dissolve itself. Thus, a genuine community effort to improve relations between the races, and between persons of different religions, was to be made a shambles by the infiltration and tactics of John Birch Society members.

Late in November, 1965, a public meeting was called in Saratoga, Calif., to discuss ways to establish an Advisory Board of Directors for an Area Center of the Poverty Program. Establishment of the Board was a necessary step toward setting up the Area Center and the meeting had been called by an ad hoc committee for the district which included more than a half-dozen communities. Close to 250 persons were present, including several prominent members of the John Birch Society in the area, and when the voting came, it appeared that at least two-thirds of the audience were Birchers or their fellow-travelers. The Birchers elected all 18 members of the Advisory Board.

A Local Front Group

The Birchers and their allies attempted takeovers, both in Mount Prospect and at Saratoga. In other communities across the nation, they have attacked on wider fronts. A case in point: Nashua, N.H. There the local Birchers operate through a front organization called the Southern New Hampshire Forum for American Opinion, Inc., which has helped fan the ideological fires by bringing to town a parade of speakers from the Birch bureau including Tom Anderson of the Birch Society Council, Julia Brown, Willis Stone, and Harold Lord Varney. They have been aided in their activities by the presence of a Nashua outlet of the "Let Freedom Ring" telephone message service which, during 1965, was warning about "treason right in the White House" and charging that the "National Council of Churches is openly promoting bloodshed through armed revolution by Negroes."

Another local outlet for the Birch line has been the Letters-to-the-Editor columns of the Manchester *Union-Leader,* which have seen long essays in thousands of words contributed by local Society members and coordinators.

Even the Rightist-oriented editorial column of *Union-Leader* editor William Loeb, however, penetrated what it called the "sham" of the Southern New Hampshire Forum's name, declaring: "This is the John Birch Society. That's a fact, not our opinion."

But another fact, not so plainly noted, was that the Young Republican organization had been infiltrated and was under Birch control. This organization, rather than the front group, brought another of the Birch bureau's speakers into the Nashua area. He was Samuel Blumenfeld, now a Western Islands editor and one of Robert Welch's "international experts," who believes that democracy is all wrong and promises it will be replaced "when and if the John Birch Society becomes a dominant political force in America."

Blumenfeld's prophecy is in words; others act. A Catholic priest in North Attleboro, Mass., who advised his parishioners not to attend a lecture by Father Francis Fenton, a member of the Birch National Council, became the target of abusive telephone calls and a whispering campaign. In Santa Barbara, Calif., a reporter who had exposed local Birch Society activities had his automobile tires slashed. The culprit is unknown.

Schools and PTA's

Birch members and other extremists use the democratic processes to harass local school boards and municipal governments.

A campaign begun by religious organizations in New Jersey to persuade schools and other municipal buildings to fly a pennant reading "One Nation Under God," together with the American Flag, aroused bitter controversies in some communities. It was seen by some as an effort to circumvent — or even to thumb the community nose at — rulings of the Supreme Court on questions of the separation of church and state. The Bergen (N.J.) *Record* disclosed that the sale of the "religious" pennants was a major local operation of Birch Society units, netting a new American Opinion bookstore in Bergen County some $200 weekly.

School boards and parent-teacher associations have been a prime target of other Radical Rightist pressures on the

47

community level in the last year or two. The National Education Association has estimated that one school district in every 30 "experienced some sort of attack, opposition or attempt to infiltrate the schools by the extremists and dissident critics."

In Carmichael, Calif., a local Birch Society member presented a petition to the school board demanding that a certain American history textbook be withdrawn as "subversive." She cited *American Opinion* poet E. Merrill Root as her expert authority. The Carmichael *Courier* reported that after her speech before the board, the lady — representing a "Committee for the Return of Morality"— screamed at the president of the local teachers' association that she would see him "burn in hell" because of his opposition to extremist views.

In 1960, Welch advised his followers to "join your local PTA at the beginning of the school year, get your conservative friends to do likewise, and go to work to take it over." Birchers around the country have been doing so, and the Society has reaped a whirlwind of adverse publicity and public hostility from mothers across the land who devote countless hours to sincere PTA work.

Rousselot's Denial

When the adverse publicity mounted, Rousselot — in February, 1965 — wrote to the Christian Science *Monitor* which had published an Associated Press dispatch under the headline "PTA Tells of Extremist Pressures." Blandly ignoring Welch's September, 1960, plea that Birchers should take over local PTAs, Rousselot admitted that members were encouraged to join PTAs, but "not because the society has any intention of taking over . . ."

Rousselot said that the Birchers wanted only to expose the PTA "to conservative thinking." He argued that "liberal elements within the PTA should welcome the ideological competition which results from contact with conservatives." Adding that the Society had "never encouraged society members to foment discord within the PTA," he said, members were counselled at all times to be "morally correct and in every way decent."

Exactly how local Birchers carried out these strictures was, perhaps, exemplified in Upper Saddle River, N.J., where Birchers, in the face of public indifference, seized control of the local PTA. While there was some indication that clashing personalities may have been involved, it was also a fact that the man who had been nominated for PTA President had been active in inter-racial activities. As the PTA election approached, he was made the subject of a whispering campaign — that he was a "nigger-lover." At the election meeting, a large proportion of Birchers and their allies were present; most PTA members were not. The Presidency and the Vice-Presidency went to Birch Society members. Happily, the publicity alerted indifferent PTA members who, in the year the Birchers held office, effectively restrained them.

Threat to PTA

This episode suggests that the Birchers can be successful not only in capturing other PTAs, but even in taking them out of the PTA national organization, as has, in fact, happened.

The Birch view of the PTA was, perhaps, spelled out in recorded telephone messages broadcast by the "Let Freedom Ring" stations often run by local Birch Society members. LFR said that the PTA was Communist-infiltrated.

National PTA President Mrs. Jennelle Moorhead reported that by early 1965, tactics of intimidation, coercion, and misrepresentation by Birchers and other extremists had become commonplace. She said that in her opinion, "these extremists are not really after the PTA but are attempting to gain control of it to get at their real objective — the educational system."

UNICEF — the UN Children Fund — is also a target of the Birchers, who have zeroed in on the Halloween "trick or treat" collections which school children make to bring in coins for UNICEF. In Needham, Mass., a local Bircher gave some children boxes of candy with a telephone number on a sticker affixed to the boxes. The number was for the local "Let Freedom Ring" Radical Right telephone message propaganda operation; those who called the number heard an attack on UNICEF and a plug for the Birch book on the UN by Griffin.

At Falmouth, Mass., on Cape Cod, a local Birch leader persuaded the Pilgrim Youth Fellowship of the First Congregational Church, consisting of high school students, to vote against supporting the 1965 UNICEF drive in the community.

Another effort by the Birchers to reach American youth took place on a national scale in the Fall of 1965. Each of the 5,000 Society chapters was asked to distribute — to college freshmen — 25 copies of *None Dare Call It Treason,* the paperback book by John Stormer, charging the national administrations of the last 30 years with treason. (The book was distributed by the millions during the 1964 Presidential election campaign by Birchers and other Radical Rightists.) In line with Welch's suggestion, Society members sent a personal note to each freshman recipient, urging that he read the Stormer book "to get some idea . . . of the true state of affairs in the world and his own country as against optimistic and deceptive twaddle he is so likely to be fed in most of the academic halls of today."

Attacks on the Press

Another American institution which has been the target of Birchers and other Radical Rightists is the nation's free press. In November, 1964, the California Newspaper Publishers Association found it necessary to launch a long-range campaign against "right-wing and left-wing attempts to discredit newspapers and other news media."

A report by a CNPA committee which studied the problem said in part:

"Members of the John Birch Society and other extreme right-wing groups have joined the long list of left-wing extremist groups which have, for at least a generation, vigorously and viciously attacked the integrity of the reporting in the press, have attempted to discredit and damage economically newspapers with which they disagree and have sought to bring into being more news media which will be subservient in reflecting their own prejudices."

The report said the attacks were particularly acute during the 1964 Presidential campaign, but added that there was "abundant evidence that the derogation [of newspapers] will not end after the election. . . ."

Two months earlier, publishers H. H. Ridder of the Long Beach *Independent* and L. Finder of the Sacramento *Union* told the Publishers Association of anti-press efforts by both extremes, but characterized the campaign of the ultra-right John Birch Society and Birch-connected affiliates as most effective and most dangerous. Jack Baldwin of the Long Beach *Independent* confirmed their findings in his report on a nationwide investigation he and a colleague had conducted over a period of eight months.

Ridder, Finder and Baldwin said the attack on the press was in two parts. First, *Editor & Publisher* reported, "is a general attack on all of the press that is not under the control of the John Birch Society. Second is the picking off of one paper at a time and attempted intimidation to force submission to the organization's dictation."

The three newsmen cited wide-ranging tactics used by extremists against the press. These included: "vituperative letters, threatening boycotts of advertisers, picketing, loading of a newspaper's mail to the point where it is unmanageable, jamming classified advertising telephone lines, and telephoned midnight threats of bodily harm to publishers, editors and their families."

Late in 1965, there began to be evidence that Birchers and other Radical Rightists in California were buying suburban dailies and weeklies, and shopping news "throwaways," in what appeared to be the beginning of an effort to build a Birchite radical rightist press network in the myriad California suburbs. In mid-1965, for example, the Downey (Calif.) *Live Wire* was sold to a group that included a John Birch Society coordinator.

'Calling All Cars'

One of the most persistent Birch Society campaigns of the last few years — and to some, one of the more alarming ones — is wrapped up in the Birch slogan, "Support Your Local Police." It is both a part of the national Birch program and an intensive local activity; it involves infiltration and it makes use of front groups; it is a holding maneuver against the enemy, a Society recruiting device, a propaganda slogan and a hullabaloo of buttons and bumper-stickers.

The campaign, begun originally in the Society's *Bulletin* of July, 1963, was obviously designed to exploit the so-called white backlash and to win friends for Welch's movement — and more particularly, to draw recruits wearing blue uniforms into the Birch chapters.

As it began, Welch declared policemen to be "the best friends everywhere of anti-Communists, like ourselves." The question that immediately arose stemmed from the Welch-Birch view of all-pervading Communism in American life. Just how would friendship with the Birch sort of "*anti*-Communist" affect the required neutrality and objectivity of law enforcement officers? For example, with respect to police handling of civil rights problems? The Birch drive had been kicked off in that first *Bulletin* with a paragraph of generous praise for the handling of Negro demonstrations by the police of Birmingham, Ala. — including their use of police dogs against peaceful demonstrators.

Hundreds of Committees

Within a year, hundreds of Committees to Support Your Local Police were established in communities all over the country. They have since distributed literally tons of Society literature and served as recruitment teams.

Through such local efforts the Birch Society has enlisted, according to publicity chief Rousselot, "growing number of police and personnel in sheriffs' departments throughout the country." Such recruitment has been pressed vigorously; in many cities its success, and the possibilities of police-Birch alliances, have become matters of deep concern.

In Santa Ana, Calif. — a city of 100,000 lying 30 miles southeast of Los Angeles — the membership of the Birch Society's Chapter QXTZ was composed of 23 city police officers. A private detective assigned by the city manager to investigate a mysterious campaign of harassment against Police Chief Edward Allen (such as anonymous telephone calls at night; an unsigned pamphlet questioning his honesty; the theft of his badges at headquarters and false alarms that dispatched fire trucks to his home) reported that the incidents had been perpetrated by members of QXTZ as a power play to get rid of a chief they did not like.

The John Birch chapter controlled the Santa Ana Police Benevolent Association, all of its officials but one being QXTZ members, and under this controlling majority the PBA by-laws were changed to enable a grievance committee to hear secret testimony against Chief Allen. One lieutenant was later dismissed from the force for engaging in Birch recruiting while on duty and for misappropriating a police vehicle. He allegedly used it while on a secret snooping mission aimed at discrediting the chief.

Other communities have witnessed what may be the beginning of a process that tears at departmental loyalties and community unity. For example:

• Two police officers in Minneapolis, one of them a deputy inspector, openly criticized the nation's courts in addresses delivered before a meeting of Birch Society members.

• In Salisbury, Mass., all persons attending the 1965 Police Association banquet on June 23 were given copies of a "Support Your Local Police" pamphlet published by the Birch Society.

• The police chief of Trenton, N. J., quoted the Society's monthly *Bulletin* verbatim in a departmental memo sent to all his men.

• James J. Allman, director of community relations for the St. Louis Police Department, resigned his position recently to become the Birch Society's paid coordinator for the state of Missouri.

• In New Jersey, State Trooper George Demetry resigned from the force to take a full-time job as a Society organizer. The State Police Superintendent said that a conference with Demetry indicated the trooper had allowed his personal philosophy to influence his professional behavior.

• In Newark, N.J., a policeman was given a three-month leave of absence to conduct Birch recruiting activities. He later went to work permanently as a Society coordinator.

• In Los Angeles, Rousselot claimed, in the Fall of 1965, that at least three district attorney's investigators, more than

53

25 policemen, about 15 sheriff's deputies and other law enforcement personnel were members of the Society.

• Official Birch material has been placed on the police
bulletin board in Rockford, Ill., and on at least one precinct
bulletin board in New York City.

• A large number of city policemen attended a rally at
New York's Town Hall auditorium in July, 1965; the rally
was sponsored by the Birch Society's American Opinion
Speakers Bureau. A New York *Post* reporter judged that the
officers, identifiable by their Police Benevolent Association
badges, made up a majority of the audience. One of the
speakers, a Birch Society Section Leader, declared: "Some
people hate the police. The Birch Society has the answer —
it is the only hope for the world."

• Mayor James H. J. Tate of Philadelphia, Pa., in plac-
ing 15 city policemen on limited duty because of their Birch
Society recruiting activities, explained: "They have limited
their capacity and usefulness to the Police Department." He
added that Birch members are, by their very membership,
"against certain groups in the big cities."

Chief William H. Parker of Los Angeles, on the other
hand, is not concerned about Society membership among his
men because the organization is "not on the subversive
list." On May 30, Chief Parker himself had appeared for an
interview on the Manion Forum, the weekly radio broadcast
of Clarence Manion, a member of the Birch Society's National Council. During that interview Parker vehemently
attacked the courts and decried a "socialistic trend" in
American life which, he charged, "involves an increased
emphasis on the rights of the individual."

Dangers

The John Birch Society is similarly concerned about the
enlargement of individual rights, especially those that have
been termed civil rights. The Society believes the civil rights
movement to have been conceived by Communists, carried
out by Communists, and controlled by Communists. This
Birch line on civil rights is one of the potential dangers of
police membership in the Birch Society.

Another danger in Birchite influence in the field of law

enforcement is the Society's view of American law itself: it preaches that much of existing law is unconstitutional and perhaps even subversive, and that the courts of the country are serving a Communist conspiracy.

Hidden Membership

Still another danger lies in the possible manipulation of the police power itself by a quasi-political force that subscribes to a strange, extremist creed and whose members take direction from a leader who controls their monolithic organization. Most important is the fact that membership in the John Birch Society (like membership in the Communist Party), is not open and above-board. It is most often secret — which means that local police departments cannot know whether any particular officer is a Society member, and whether he may therefore have divided loyalties.

Commenting on police membership in the Birch Society, Mayor Tate remarked: "This is the way the Nazi Party began."

Though the Society has had only limited success in infiltration so far, the value of the "Support your Local Police" campaign for purposes of public image, and as an aid in general recruiting, should not be underestimated.

The real significance of the campaign, however, lies perhaps in its implication for the civil rights movement. For Welch began it — at least in the pages of the Birch Society *Bulletin* — with the situation in Birmingham, where the police and civil rights workers were clearly squared off against each other. The implication was that civil rights activity was a lawless cause, quite aside from the Birch charge that it is controlled by Communists.

55

6   *Public Relations*

During the period of its recent membership growth the Society began to use modern public relations techniques to change its public image. The Society is seeking to lose the flavor of secrecy and irresponsible extremism and to develop an aura of respectability. It is striving to portray itself as a group of conservative, patriotic citizens, dedicated to saving the Republic from the Communist influence it says pervades all aspects of American life, an influence aided and abetted by five Presidents, by cabinet members, judges and other national leaders.

Sen. Goldwater's ringing defense of extremism at the 1964 Republican National Convention helped start the image change, giving to extremists of the Radical Right a degree of respectability which aided their growth in the months that followed. And the Society itself began a major effort that very same summer with the establishment of its own Public Relations Department.

To head the campaign, Welch chose former Rep. John H. Rousselot, a California Republican and a personable public relations man, who had served for almost two years as the Society's Western States "Governor" following his 1962 defeat in a bid for re-election to Congress as one of the two known Birchers in the lower House.

Rousselot, whose "Beliefs and Principles of the John Birch Society" — after being entered into the *Congressional*

Record — became a standard Society leaflet, is assisted by Regional Public Relations Managers — one in the East, one in the Midwest, one in the Southwest, and one in Washington, D.C. Thomas Davis, a former major coordinator, is the Eastern Manager for public relations, working out of the recently-established Society office in White Plains, N.Y. Roger Morrison, an attractive young man, is Midwest Manager and makes his headquarters at the new Society office at Glenview, Ill., just outside Chicago. Rex Westerfield is in charge of the Southwest and is based in Dallas. Reed Benson, the Society's Washington, D.C. representative, handles public relations in the Capital, working out of the new Society office there.

Rousselot's headquarters is at San Marino, Calif., a wealthy Los Angeles suburb, but he makes frequent trips to oversee the regional offices, and spends a good deal of time at Belmont, just as Welch spends increasing time in California.

Birch Society public relations ranges from the sublime — the colorful and thoroughly professional Sunday news supplement — to the ridiculous, the Society's telephone number at its Washington office being "1984."

The Birch Sunday Supplement

The expensive, multi-colored 16-page Sunday Supplement was Rousselot's first major project as Public Relations Director of the Society. Printed by rotogravure with negatives supplied by Birch headquarters itself, the Supplement soft-pedals Welch's wild charges against President Eisenhower and other American leaders of the last three decades. Ignoring the more extreme Birch positions on public affairs, the Supplement portrays the Society as a polished, responsible, advisory council of dedicated, prominent, patriotic citizens of conservative viewpoint whose only aim is to fight Communism and to restore high moral, civic and religious idealism to America.

While the Supplement was written by the Society's headquarters under Rousselot's supervision, it is printed locally and the cost in each city is borne by local Birch members and wealthy supporters who often make their contributions anonymously.

How come the Rich wan't To save this Country from Communism

57

The Supplement first appeared in September, 1964, in the Los Angeles *Times* and the Los Angeles *Herald Examiner*. The cost was about $75,000. An additional $25,000 reportedly was spent on radio and other promotion — a total cost of almost $100,000, contributed by a wealthy Californian.

The Supplement was placed in some 16 leading newspapers such as the Chicago *Tribune,* the Detroit *Free Press,* the Boston *Herald* (which gave the proceeds to charity while criticizing the Society), the Pittsburgh *Press,* the St. Louis *Globe-Democrat,* the Milwaukee *Journal,* the Indianapolis *Times,* and the Dallas *Morning News*. In Houston, copies of the Supplement were mailed directly to individual homes, addressed merely to "Occupant."

The authoritative *Advertising Age* reported that during 1964, the John Birch Society spend $305,475 for advertising space.

Words of Praise

In its effort to create a more respectable image, one page in the Supplement carries photographs of well-known Americans, quoting each in a few good words for the Birch organization. Included are Sen. Strom Thurmond (R., S.C.) ; Tom Anderson, a member of the Society's own National Council; Rev. J. L. Ward, a Negro Birch ally; and former Secretary of Agriculture Ezra Taft Benson, who served in the Eisenhower Cabinet and whose son, Reed, is the Society's Washington, D.C. representative.

On the following page there appears the picture and a laudatory quote from an "ordinary" member — the only one so honored. She is identified as Mrs. Beth Cleminson of San Gabriel, Calif., who explains in the quotation why she joined the Society. Persons who have corresponded with the Society's office in San Marino, Calif., recognize Mrs. Cleminson's name. She is secretary to Rousselot.

Indicative of the techniques employed in the Society's public relations project for 1964 was the use — in the original Los Angeles version of the Supplement — of the pictures of Dwight Eisenhower and J. Edgar Hoover, each accompanied by a quotation apparently praising the John Birch Society. Welch's characterization of Gen. Eisenhower as "a dedicated, conscious agent of the Communist conspiracy" was

58

by that time a matter of public knowledge all across the country. The former President's public expression of distaste for the Society, and its attempt to use his name, forced a change in the Supplement. All reference to him was deleted. Said Eisenhower:

"I have no respect whatsoever for that individual or for anyone else who associates himself with such unconscionable practices."

As for FBI Director Hoover, the anti-Communist quotation attributed to him had been made many years earlier in a statement to a Congressional committee. Later versions of the Supplement indicated that the Hoover quotation should not be viewed as an endorsement of the Birch Society; apparently protests must have been registered here too.

'The Politician' Problem

Welch's charge that President Eisenhower was an agent of Communism has been one of the most serious problems that has faced the Society. It has caused considerable chagrin to its constituency, some of whom have stated publicly that they do not agree on that point with the man whose leadership they follow dutifully and who runs the monolithic Society with a firm hand.

Rousselot was quoted in the Sacramento *Bee* of April 11, 1965 as stating publicly that Welch had been right about Eisenhower. On the other hand, he has tried to disassociate the Society from the extremist views of Welch on the subject of President Eisenhower, Milton Eisenhower, the late John Foster Dulles, and ex-CIA Chief Allen Dulles, all of whom were branded as agents of Communism by Welch in his notorious book, *The Politician.*

In a June 22, 1965, press release, Rousselot quoted Welch as stating:

"Neither The John Birch Society nor its members have ever had any connection with *The Politician* in any way. . . ."

The statement was less than completely candid. *The Politician,* expurgated, has received widespread distribution through the organized efforts of Society officials and Society members ever since Welch published it. The cleansed version which appeared in early 1963 contained softer language about President Eisenhower. But it did not alter the basic thrust that the former President was a Communist agent. (Society members were never explicitly told that the published version differed in its text from the original, although an explanation was included in the revised text. Instead they — and the public — were told to "Read It and Judge For Yourself"— as if the readers were getting the original version.)

Not only are individual Birchers active in distributing *The Politician.* It is sold in every American Opinion bookstore. It is advertised in Birch Society publications. It is loaned to new members by the chapters, each of which receives a free copy. It has been recommended in the Birch *Bulletin* as a tool for recruiting, and it is promoted at Birch meetings and rallies.

A Measure of Success

Recently, Welch described the United States as "an insane asylum, run by its worst patients." Yet the Society has had a measure of success in its efforts to improve its image and achieve a measure of respectability. Rousselot, Davis and the other public relations men — clean-cut, conservative-looking, button-down shirt types — have made themselves more easily accessible and available to the press, to radio and to TV. When they do not have to debate well-informed opponents, and can expound dedicated patriotism and anti-Communism without having to cope with the problem of Welch's extremism, they come across to the average listener as mere conservatives. When pressed, however, they are the prisoners of the real Birch line that the nation is well down the road to Communism and that the whole American society is heavily infested with Communistic influences.

A stable of Birchite speakers has brought the Birch line to college campuses, local civic associations, service clubs and veterans' organizations. The Birchers take booths at state and county fairs. There was a Birch booth at the 10-day Illinois State Fair in 1965, and at some dozen county fairs in that state alone. Local chapters have entered patriotic floats in many a holiday parade; some have even won prizes.

In at least one California community, the Chamber of

Commerce lists the Birch cell as a recognized community organization. National Council member Tom Anderson spoke at the Americanism program of the DeMotte, Ind., American Legion post, in April, 1965, and Council member Clarence Manion was a featured speaker at the convention of the California Real Estate Association in September, 1965. When an American Opinion bookstore was opened last year in the Milwaukee suburb of Wauwatosa, its Mayor, Ervin A. Meier, personally cut the tape at a formal ceremony attended by Welch.

Continuing Problems

Yet the Society remains trapped, in its efforts to build a better image, by its own extremism, by the activities already mentioned of some of its members in making anti-Semitic materials available at American Opinion bookstores, and by a lack of public relations sense on the part of some of its officials.

For example, although Welch announced back in 1963 that he had revoked the membership of Robert De Pugh, gun-toting leader of the para-military Minutemen, the Kansas City *Star* reported on September 16, 1965 that when De Pugh addressed a local "conservative" group in August, he had been introduced by James Kernodle, a Kansas City section leader of the Birch Society.

Again, when Reed Benson opened the Washington, D.C. office in September, 1965, reporters asked whether he thought President Johnson to be guilty of treasonable acts. Benson replied:

"The Constitution defines treason as giving aid and comfort to the enemy, and I believe we are giving aid and comfort to the enemy. What do you call it?"

An Embarrassing Episode

Toward the end of 1965, the Birch Society was confronted with an embarrassing public relations problem — right in its own New England back yard. A local Birch leader in Middleboro, Mass., inserted an ad in a local paper, announcing a Society meeting. The ad quoted six lines from a letter written some years ago by Richard Cardinal Cushing of Boston in which he had praised Welch and endorsed

61

the Society — a letter whose content the Cardinal had later repudiated.

When Cardinal Cushing learned that his old letter was again being used by Birch Society members, he wrote Welch to protest:

"It is happening again and again. Your field agents . . . use a letter I sent years ago. . . .

"What am I to do with regard to having my name misused in this fashion? You know that I have absolutely nothing to do with the John Birch Society — I was never a member of it and I simply cannot understand the means this organization uses in recruiting members. . . .

"If I had had this ad in my hands last Saturday, I would have had every Catholic Church in the neighborhood announce on the following day that they were to disregard this publicity in its entirety and at the same time advise the Catholic people that I have no respect for or confidence in those behind the Middleboro Branch of the John Birch Society.

"I have yet to find a member of the Society whom I would trust as a result of the way its leaders have used a letter I sent years ago to some one in California in which I paid you a high personal tribute. What a fool I was to put in writing my one time admiration and affection for you."

Leo Kahian, the Middleboro Birch leader responsible for the ad, said later he had made a mistake in quoting the old letter by the Cardinal and that he had not known that the Society warned all chapters in May, 1964, not to use it.

The Boston Sunday *Herald* reported that Welch had sent a letter of apology to Cardinal Cushing, but the publication in the same paper of the Cardinal's sharp letter to Welch did nothing to enhance the Society's image in the heavily Catholic areas of New England.

Public Relations and Recruiting

Public relations techniques aid Birch Society recruiting, but are not a substitute for the actual, continuing, recruitment program being carried out by the Society. The 75 coordinators in the field, backstopped by a team at headquarters who supervise various geographical areas of the country, are the heart of the Birch Society's organizing apparatus. They are the key to keeping existing chapters hewing to the Birch line and working full blast on Society projects, and to organizing new chapters as well.

It costs the Society roughly $15,000 to put a new coordinator into the field, including his first year's salary and the books and equipment he needs, such as films, projectors, and tape recorders. The 35 coordinators who have been added to the Society's staff in the last 18-24 months, therefore, represent an investment by the Society of about half-a-million dollars. But to put new salesmen into the field requires a steady and growing reservoir of capital to sustain them during the training and initial period of work — until they organize enough new chapters to achieve a kind of self-supporting status through the dollar inflow which new members supply. Which is why Welch, Rousselot and the Society's professional staff, aided by National Council members and key supporters across the country, devote a major part of their time to fund-raising.

7

Political Crash Program

Immediately after the 1964 election campaign, Welch began looking ahead to the needs and goals of the Society for 1965 and 1966. The focus — and the target — was to be 1966 which offered the convenient horizon of another nationwide march to the polls to elect members of Congress.

In March, 1965, Welch sought to launch a crash program of massive fund-raising which he outlined in a 24-page booklet entitled *Looking Ahead*. Its target audience was wealthy business men who had previously helped the Society with contributions. The appeal was "hard sell" and Welch set forth his goals plainly. He proposed to double the Society's size in 1965 as he had in 1964, and to redouble it in 1966. The reason: to influence the outcome of the 1966 Congressional elections. The method: the placement of 1000 Birch members — 50 chapters — in each of 325 Congressional Districts to act as "ideological salesmen" and to help elect "conservative" candidates. Needed to do the job: working capital in the amount of $6 million for 1965 and $12 million in 1966.

In setting the target of doubling in 1965 and redoubling in 1966, Welch wrote that "there is nothing to prevent our achieving this rate of growth during both years except the money to finance it. But a geometric expansion of our size and influence requires a geometric expansion of income running ahead of it."

New Capital Needed

New capital was needed also for an increase in publishing activities, for new films and projectors, for the whole-

64

sale service to bookstores, for expansion of *American Opinion* and the speakers' bureau, and for "more supervisory help than we have ever had before."

Welch pleaded for a prompt influx of big money "through the following sources or channels:

"1. Direct contributions to the John Birch Society . . .

"2. Purchases of our publications, to be distributed either by the purchaser or by ourselves in accordance with the purchaser's specifications . . .

"3. Loans to *American Opinion* at five percent interest, with either a three-year or a five-year maturity . . ."

"We are facing up squarely to a . . . supremely important undertaking," Welch continued. "So we are talking about a lot of money, and the sums now required may seem frighteningly large."

That was March, 1965. By July, Welch had to admit the crash fund-raising was — at least temporarily — a failure. And to all the members then came a nine-page letter, originally intended for a mere 50 persons in the "big money" class, and printed under the title, *A Stick of Dynamite* (to blast "apathetic minds"). The new appeal put a frank $3 million "price tag" on the Birch program for the immediate future. "Or, in simple language," Welch wrote in July, "we have to raise three million dollars, over and above the normal flow of money from our membership at large — and we have to raise it now."

Concerning his *Looking Ahead* appeal four months earlier, Welch wrote that "for whatever reason we do not know, that pamphlet brought us very little of the 'big money' needed to carry out its projected accomplishment." Now, the "big money" was to be blasted out by Welch's dynamite "with great regret but no apology" — and potential contributors were informed plainly that "checks may be made out to The John Birch Society, or to *American Opinion,* or to *Correction, Please!,* or to Escrow Account No. 78. They may be sent as straight contributions or, if preferred in the case of larger amounts, as five-year loans to *American Opinion* at five percent interest to serve our urgent need for working capital."

(The Escrow Account No. 78 is probably an account maintained by the Society for contributors who do not

65

wish to draw their checks openly to the order of an identifiable Birch Society operation. The "78" apparently was taken from the Society's old postal zone number — Belmont 78, Mass.")

Circumstantial Evidence

There is no certain way of telling exactly how successful Welch was with his second "Stick of Dynamite" appeal for big money. But circumstantial evidence clearly indicates that it achieved enough to make possible the expansion of the Society in the second half of 1965. One source of money which the Society tapped with apparent success was the Testimonial Dinner for Founder Welch himself. At least five such affairs were held in various cities — Los Angeles, Phoenix, Dallas, New York and Chicago — and the gross was more than $200,000. The charge was $25 a plate in Phoenix, Dallas and Chicago; and $50 a plate in Los Angeles and New York.

Phoenix drew 1100 persons, Dallas, 1000, Los Angeles, 1700, New York, 1100, and Chicago, 750 — which adds up to a total of $211,250.

Birchers in New York were under the most intense pressure to attend. Because of the high price per plate, credit was extended to members — a kind of "testimonial dine now and pay later" plan that made it hard for members to say no.

The best evidence that Welch's hard-sell fund-raising appeals of March and July, 1965, and the testimonial dinners, brought in the necessary funds can be seen in just a few financial details he disclosed. By year's end, he was boasting that the Society was spending $125,000 a month for printing alone — up $40,000 a month. New co-ordinators were added to the Birch staff — ten or twelve men. Other arms of the apparatus, such as Western Islands and the Research Dept., appeared to be operating with more personnel. The payroll, which Welch put at the $30,000-a-week level in March, climbed to $40,000 by year's end — an approximate annual increase of more than half-a-million dollars.

Quite aside from operating expenditures, the Society has problems of capital outlay — for miscellaneous office and shipping room machinery, for new office equipment, for new films and projectors for the army of coordinators and section leaders. What it all added up to was a need — and a drive — to raise an additional $3,000,000 during 1965. By the end of the year, it seemed clear that the Birchers were spending $6,000,000 a year — or almost — and in November, Welch was running an operation spending more than $100,000 a week.

But even more significant was the openly political purpose for which the fund-raising and intensified recruitment drives were mounted. The target was the 1966 Congressional elections. Welch is aiming at nothing less than changing the political complexion of the United States Congress by mobilizing local Birch power to influence voting results at the local level. The whole crash program of fund-raising is, in fact, tied to the need for more recruiting, and the need for recruiting is tied by Welch to the political goal.

He spelled it out plainly in *Looking Ahead*:

"There are 435 Congressional Districts in the United States. Except in extremely rare instances and under the most unusual circumstances, there is no doubt that one hundred chapters of The John Birch Society, in any Congressional District, can exercise enough influence over political thinking within that district to control the political action there. And this would be done, without the Society itself ever endorsing a candidate, or taking any direct action in politics; but simply by our members proceeding on their own initiative from the basic principles and purposes of the Society, and persuading others to do the same . . .

"As a practical matter, therefore, let's consider what we could do with 50 chapters per district in 75% of the Congressional Districts in the whole United States . . .

"Now our chapters average about twenty members each. This means that we are talking about a working force of one thousand members for each Congressional District . . .

"Think of your own Congressional District and imagine one thousand truly informed and deeply dedicated neighborhood, community, and regional leaders, ceaselessly at work — nights as well as days, and weekends as well as nights — to inform and convince their fellow citizens."

The transparently political goal tended to surprise those who had listened for several years to the bland assurances of Welch, Rousselot and other Birch spokesmen, protesting that the John Birch Society was a non-political organization, and that its members were free to support whomever they wished in elections.

The Political Cadre

But it should not be forgotten that the Society is a political cadre of thoroughly indoctrinated, zealous and dedicated activists. As the Communists considered themselves the vanguard of the proletariat — of the Radical Left — so Robert Welch views his body of men and women as the vanguard and the elite leadership corps of the Radical Right. And just as the Communist goal was — and is — political power, so too, the ultimate goal of the Birch Society is political power.

Both concentrate on propaganda and recruitment, on getting their message to enough people to recruit a strong cadre to their ranks. This is called "education," whether it is carried out by the Radical Left or the Radical Right. But when the cadre is built, and as it keeps growing, the process of infiltration and penetration into the vital organs of the target society begins to take place. Sometimes candidates are nominated, and a few even elected. But the cadre does not really expect to win many contests at the polls. Political activity is a vehicle for propaganda and recruitment, and an instrument for building the movement to larger proportions. Years ago, Welch had this to say — as the tenth point in his program for launching the Society:

"Finally, and probably most important of all these courses of action, we would put our weight into the political scales in this country just as fast and far as we could. For unless we can eventually, and in time, reverse by political action the gradual surrender of the United States to Communism, the ultimate alternative of reversal by military uprising is fearful to contemplate."

Welch went on to explain why the country could not be saved by the Republican Party alone, or by political leaders (including Barry Goldwater) in the Republican Party. The Republican Party, he said, could not win *"unless* it has strong help and backing from forces outside of the straight political organization — such as the Democratic Party has on the other side in Walter Reuther's Committee on Political Education."

Welch added (and repeated in the Fall of 1964 — after the Presidential election) :

"We are at a stage, gentlemen, where the only sure political victories are achieved by non-political organization; by organization which has a surer, more positive, and more permanent purpose than the immediate political goals that are only a means to an end; by organization which has a backbone, and cohesiveness and strength, and definiteness of direction which are impossible for the old-style political party organization . . .

"We would have to move into this field, gentlemen, with a body of our own. . . . But with a million men and the resources consistent with the dedication of those men which we are presupposing, we could move in on the elections thereafter with both more man power and more resources than Reuther will be able to marshal by that time."

There is little doubt that when Welch formed the Birch Society at Indianapolis in 1958, he believed he would have no special problem in mobilizing a million members in due course — and certainly far before 1966. Today, he is still struggling below the 100,000 mark. But this obvious failure should blind no one to the essential and ultimate goal of the Society — political influence and power. That fight the Birch Society has not yet lost.

All Birch activity since 1958 has been, then, a necessary prelude to the achievement of political influence and power. The 1966 objectives of the Society — short run objectives, in plain fact — are merely a step on a longer road. And despite the unprecedented volume of criticism that has been directed at Welch and his Society in recent years — dating back to 1960 when Welch's manuscript on Eisenhower was exposed by the American press — the John Birch Society has come a good piece down the road its Founder has set for it.

8

The JBS
and the GOP

In the Birch Society's penetration of American Society, the single most important step has been the infiltration of the Republican Party by Welch's dedicated and indoctrinated cadres.

The ordeal of the Republican Party in its struggle with the intrusion of extremism in its ranks has been a matter of public record since the 1964 GOP convention at the Cow Palace in San Francisco. The problem existed when the delegates convened. (The Birchers claim that some 100 delegates and alternates in San Francisco were Birch Society members.) It grew during the campaign period when the Birchers, on the heels of Sen. Goldwater's ringing defense of extremism, moved into the campaign and used it as a vehicle for their own special purposes of propaganda and recruitment. Birchers moved into the Party in increasing numbers, and some party members moved into the Birch Society in a cross-fertilization whose results have been apparent ever since: fattened Society strength and greater Birchite influence at the grass-roots levels of the GOP itself.

The event that apparently led to a move, late in 1965, for a Republican Party repudiation of the John Birch Society was the entry of Bircher Richard Murphy into the Republican primary against incumbent Sen. Karl Mundt, of South Dakota, a staunch Republican conservative. Murphy announced he would challenge Mundt for the nomination on September 8, 1965. He conceded that Mundt was a conservative, but said the Senator had been far too liberal in his votes supporting farm price support programs, civil rights, foreign aid, and federal aid to education.

The Morton Statement

Less than a month later, Sen. Thruston Morton of Kentucky, former GOP National Chairman and himself a moderate conservative, declared in Washington:

"As a partisan Republican, I am concerned by the fact that the John Birch Society has picked my party . . . as the vehicle to promulgate its monolithic philosophy.

"There are three organizations in this country which give me grave doubts as a citizen: the Communist Party, the Ku Klux Klan, and the John Birch Society. Although their goals differ, they have one thing in common, and that is secrecy . . .

"During the 1940s, the Communist Party tried to infiltrate the great Democratic Party. They didn't do it . . .

"What really concerns me is that a secret society should threaten and attempt to destroy one of our two great political parties. The Birchites label the late John Foster Dulles and Dr. Milton Eisenhower as Communists. They label General Dwight Eisenhower as a Communist sympathizer. They imply that Barry Goldwater is a Socialist. In my book, these men are great Americans. I don't think we have any room in the Republican Party for a clandestine organization engaged in character assassination."

Morton was also quoted as saying that "it's not the Birch membership I'm aiming at. Most of the members would be welcome into the Republican Party. But the leadership takes over the party at the precinct level. This is a threat to our party . . . you have to think their way — or you are out. They take over the precinct organization and if you are not with them, you are out."

The Kentucky Senator gave an example of what scared him:

"I was talking to a John Bircher out in Illinois. He asked me, 'How are we going to get rid of Percy (Charles Percy, GOP candidate for Governor of Illinois in 1964 and chairman of Bell and Howell), that Communist, and Dirksen, that Socialist?' Have you ever heard such nonsense?

"So I asked him: 'What are you doing to get rid of Mayor Richard Daley (of Chicago) and other Democratic leaders?' He answered: 'I'm not worrried about them. I just want to get Percy and Dirksen out of the party.' "

A day later, Morton was joined in his denunciation by Dirksen, the Senate minority leader, and by Rep. Gerald Ford, the House minority leader. A number of other Republican leaders issued statements — Gov. Mark Hatfield of Oregon, Sen. Jacob Javits of New York, Sen. Leverett Saltonstall of Massachusetts and others.

The Bliss Statement

On November 5, 1965, at an Albuquerque news conference, Republican National Chairman Ray Bliss called on all Republicans to "reject membership in any radical organization which attempts to use the Republican Party for its own ends." Mr. Bliss did not identify the groups he referred to, but he specifically berated Welch in expressing concern about "extremism of the radical right." He said "honest, patriotic and conscientious conservatives may be misjudged because of irresponsible radicals such as Robert Welch."

The reaction of the Birch leaders was predictable. The attacks, they said, were part of the Communist conspiracy. Welch strongly implied that Morton, Dirksen, Ford and the other GOP spokesmen were victims of Red plotting. When asked specifically if they were, he replied to newsmen:

"Through three or four removed developments — absolutely." He observed that "Lenin said Communism had been made successful by non-Communist hands" and added that 95% of those who carry out the Communist goals "don't even know it."

(On several other occasions, Welch wisecracked that when the Birchers were accused of "stealing the Republican Party" they were in fact being charged with "petty larceny.")

'Bilderbergers'

Rousselot stated darkly that Rep. Ford was a member of "one of the most highly active left-wing groups in the

72

country — the DeBilderberger (sic) group — which meets clandestinely." He said that Ford, generally considered a conservative, should be asked about the group.

(The Bilderberger group is sponsored by Crown Prince Bernhard of The Netherlands and is an unofficial, changing assemblage of leaders from Atlantic Community nations who meet twice a year to discuss world problems. They first met in 1954 and took their name from their first meeting place, the Bilderberg Hotel at Oosterbeek, The Netherlands. Leaders who join in the discussions don't belong to the group, but are invited by Bernhard to attend. Radical Right propagandists view the Bilderberger group as "secret kingmakers" and as "a little clique of powerful men (who) meet secretly and plan events that appear to have 'just happened.' " They see it as the heart, so to speak, of some secret and clandestine international conspiracy for a "one world government" in which the powerful "Eastern Establishment" in the United States plays a leading role. Some of those, besides Congressman Ford, who have attended include former Secretary of State Christian Herter, Secretary of State Dean Rusk, Gen. Alfred Gruenther, Gen. Lyman Lemnitzer, Paul-Henri Spaak of Belgium, Guy Mollet of France, Hugh Gaitskell of Great Britain, and Per Jacobsson, world-famous Swedish economist. As Rep. Ford pointed out, "they don't put out any releases" and he added, they don't do anything but talk. They make no decisions, he said, cast no votes, and have no power or standing.)

Rousselot's Statement

On October 29, in Washington, as the tide of criticism against the Birch Society mounted in Republican circles, Rousselot held a news conference at which he denied that the Society was trying to take over the Republican Party. "We have no program of infiltration," he said. "We leave that up to individual members." He said he was glad the Republican critics of the Society had made it clear that the John Birch Society "is not part of the Republican Party because we are not."

Rousselot added the standard Birch Society line:

"We are not a part of any political party, and we are not a political party ourselves. We don't endorse candidates and we don't make campaign contributions. We are primarily an educational institution. But we do encourage our members to take an active interest in the party of their choice."

He said that "while we have no program of taking over either party, both parties are beginning to feel the impact of our program."

Rousselot said the Society's membership was about evenly divided between Republicans and Democrats and that about 20% of the Democratic members lived in the South. (Some time later, the New York *Herald Tribune* tartly commented that "it may be true that half, more or less, of the John Birch Society are Democrats, but the Republican Party is still the one hung with the Birch albatross." The newspaper added: "Whether fairly or not, the GOP is the one that has to dissociate itself specifically and unequivocally from the paranoid idiocies of the Boston candy-maker and his misled followers.")

Welch's Statement

The Rousselot news conference delineated the Birch public relations position, but in the November, 1965, monthly *Bulletin* of the Society, Welch charged that the outbreak of "Birch-baiting" was Communist-inspired. Recalling his standard line — that the Communists on orders from Moscow had been trying to destroy the Society since 1960 — Welch wrote that "the Communists have now inspired, initiated, created and unleashed a campaign of attack against The John Birch Society that makes all earlier attacks look like mere pilot operations."

He added:

"Lenin said that Communism must always be advanced primarily by non-Communist hands. The Communists have always followed . . . that principle. So most of the attack against us, which is now in a crescendo movement, is by good people who have no idea that somehow they have been beguiled into carrying the ball for the Communists and doing the comrades' dirty work. Some who add their contributions to the campaign are simply opportunists. And there is no doubt that most politicians certainly do wish we would go away, and let

74

them have the political field to play games according to their own rules of expediency."

(A *New York Times* report on the conflict between the GOP and the Society compared the Birch reaction to that of the Communists in the 1930s who cried "red-baiting" whenever their role in the liberal movement of that day was exposed.)

Welch advised his followers not to "get bogged down, and waste our time and our energy, in defending ourselves; in refuting this falsehood and explaining that distortion and answering some malicious accusation — for that is exactly what the Communists want us to do!" He told his followers to leave it to Rousselot and the PR department to handle the job of setting the record straight and not fall into the trap. He reminded them that "it is because we have never fallen into this trap, but have gone right ahead working on our own plans and purposes, that we have grown steadily through such a ceaseless continuum of vicious attacks, to reach our present size, effectiveness — and a position to endanger a major plank in the foundation of the Communist program."

A Full-Page Ad

The attacks from Republican sources jolted the Society enough for the leaders of the Birch movement to produce a full-page advertisement, intended for insertion by local Birchers around the country, which bore the headline: "What Is The John Birch Society? — The Truth May Surprise You!"

The ad reviewed the history of the Society, told of its growth, claimed that this growth had led to a Communist decision to destroy the Society, and had stirred up "the politicians" who were, in effect, "running interference for the Communists." It reviewed the accomplishments of the Society, pointing with pride to the obsolete 1963 report of the California Senate's Fact-Finding Committee on Un-American Activities, and denied any similarity between the Society and the Communists in aims or tactics. It ended with an appeal to readers to "join us *now* in our epic undertaking."

There were two significant aspects to the Birch ad. The

75

first was that Welch's name did not appear in it. Instead, it was signed by the four-man Executive Committee of the Society — William J. Grede, chairman, of Milwaukee, Laurence Bunker of Wellesley, Mass., A. G. Heinsohn, Jr., of Sevierville, Tenn., and Robert W. Stoddard of Worcester, Mass.

The second significant aspect of the ad was its timing.

Timing

Mailed out on glossy paper, suitable for photo-engraving on short notice, with the December, 1965, issue of the Birch *Bulletin* in the first week of that month, the ad was timed for publication around the country at the very juncture when the Republican Coordinating Committee was to meet in Washington on December 13, to consider, among other things, a resolution repudiating the Society.

In the *Bulletin,* Welch described the ad as a "report to the nation" on the Society's seventh anniversary. He said he hoped it could be published in papers around the country, "preferably on Thursday, December 9th . . ." Welch told his members that if that could be done, "it would be quite effective as a constructive presentation of the Society to the public view," adding "And we know that it would serve some other very important purposes which would take too long to explain fully here."

The ad quickly appeared in the Chicago *Tribune,* the St. Louis *Globe-Democrat,* and many other papers in various parts of the country. Welch urged that no money earmarked for direct contribution to the Society be diverted to the cost of publishing the ad.

When the GOP Coordinating Committee met in Washington on December 13, it adopted a resolution which did not name the John Birch Society specifically but which endorsed the position taken by Bliss at Albuquerque. It called on all Republicans to "reject membership in any radical or extremist organization including any which attempts to use the Republican party for its own ends or any which seeks to undermine the basic principles of American freedom and constitutional government."

Rousselot quickly announced the Society was "pleased" by the GOP stand. He said it was "wise of the Republican Party to make it clear that it doesn't seem to be influenced by extremist groups such as the Communist party or the Ku Klux Klan." The Birch spokesman said it would have been a mistake to include the Birch Society in the resolution "because the Society wants to strengthen constitutional government and in no way has attempted to use the Republican Party for its own ends."

Republican Answers

This brought reaction from key members of the GOP group. Congressman Ford said Rousselot hadn't understood the meaning of the resolution. Gov. Robert Smylie of Idaho, who had pressed for a stronger resolution specifically naming the Birch Society, said the framers had intended that the Birch Society *would* be covered by the wording. So did Gov. George Romney of Michigan who, with Gov. John A. Love of Colorado, had at the last minute reportedly opposed naming the Society.

The New York Times, quoting "informed sources" on the subject, said the compromise resolution was proposed after Bliss had warned Smylie and others favoring stronger wording that the language they sought would antagonize a number of major contributors.

The New York *Herald Tribune,* in an editorial captioned "Sparing The Birch Rod" commented on December 15, that the GOP Coordinating Committee had "fumbled." It called the resolution "patently futile" and declared: "The responsibility of political leaders is not merely to denounce sin, but to identify the sinners — or at least specify the sin."

It added that it was not so much "the outside activities of individual Republicans" with which the GOP unit should have been concerned, as it was "the outside (i.e. Birch) organizational efforts to penetrate, capture and subvert the party."

The *Herald Tribune* concluded that "the committee's retreat was an abject failure of leadership, and dismal evidence that the lessons of 1964 have still not been learned."

California Problem

The party's difficulties are both national and local. Penetration by Birchers into the vital organs of the Republican organization at the grass-roots level has created problems in a number of states. The penetration of the party by Birchers was most acute in California where it has rocked the GOP organization for many months and still colors much of the political picture in the nation's biggest state. The loosely-structured Republican organization in California made penetration by the Birchers relatively easy and also gave them an influence far out of proportion to their numbers. This was especially true because they are an ideologically-united faction which knows what it wants, which has a single-minded purpose and outlook, and which faces a divided and somewhat confused opposition of Republican conservatives, moderates and liberals.

In the contest for the GOP gubernatorial nomination that was shaping up all during 1965, with Ronald Reagan, a Goldwater Republican, as a leading contender, the Birch issue was Topic A through most of the year. In California:

• Local Republican clubs from time to time invite Birchite speakers to address them.

• Rousselot, himself, perhaps the Number Two professional Bircher in the country, held a seat on the Los Angeles County Central Republican Committee. (There were moves by anti-Birch Republicans to oust him.)

• An official of the United Republicans of California, composed mostly of traditional conservative Republicans, said the group included in its membership 10% to 15% who were either Birch members or Birch sympathizers.

• The 13,500 member California Young Republican organization, early in 1965, adopted a resolution attacking Chief Justice Earl Warren and the Supreme Court and, while the resolution did not call for Warren's impeachment, it did call on the Congress to take "corrective action."

• In October, 1965, the Los Angeles County Young Republicans went on record in defense of the Birch Society, shouting approval of a resolution which expressed "confidence that the John Birch Society is composed of loyal and concerned Americans." (The action came only a few days after national Republican leaders Morton, Dirksen, and Ford criticized the Birchers and urged repudiation of the Society by the National GOP leadership. At the same time, the President of the California Republican Assembly defended the Birchers against the attacks by the national GOP leaders.)

Some at the meeting of the Los Angeles Young Republican group argued that the pro-Birch resolution was an act of "political suicide." Likewise, the President of the California Federation of Republican Women accused the Birchers of pursuing "divisive tactics" within the GOP and the women's organization.

By the end of 1965, the Republicans in California were still torn and divided by the Birch issue, and it was causing leaders and candidates there — not to mention the party itself — a major headache. It also seemed clear that the issue itself would figure heavily in the 1966 state campaign.

North Dakota and Washington

In North Dakota, Bircher Martin Vaaler was already campaigning in the Fall of 1965 for the Republican Congressional nomination to oppose incumbent Democrat Rep. Roland Redlin. North Dakota Birchers were, moreover, in a noisy quarrel with Republican Sen. Milton Young and Republican State Chairman T. L. Secrest.

In the State of Washington the problem of Birch penetration in the GOP became, during 1965, serious enough for Republican Gov. Dan Evans to levy a major attack on the Society at a meeting of the State's Republican Central Committee, held in September at Port Angeles. The Governor's attack formed the basis for a resolution, repudiating the Birchers. But shortly after the resolution was adopted, it became clear that there was to be no mass ouster of Birch members from Republican ranks, even though the Society had been a bone sticking in the throat of the party and the Governor's administration for a full year. The Seattle *Times* of September 22, 1965, quoted GOP State Chairman C. Montgomery Johnson as saying:

"We intend that spokesmen for the Republicans can express conservative views without being labeled extremists. It shouldn't be necessary for conservatives to preface their remarks by stating that they are not Birchers."

79

Johnson said the Washington State GOP had no intention of purging Birch members from its ranks and that the resolution at Port Angeles was designed to inform the general public that the Republican Party could not and would not be held responsible for positions taken by the Birch Society leadership. (In Spokane, meantime, the Spokane Women's Republican Club voted to defy the State Federation of Women's Republican Clubs and show a Birch Society film "if the opportunity presents itself.")

The Republican Party's problem in Washington was Birch infiltration in 10 or more of the State's 39 counties. In recent years there have been reports of some degree of Birch penetration in Republican organizations in such states as Michigan, Texas, Indiana, Illinois, Nebraska, the Dakotas, Arizona, Maryland and the District of Columbia, and throughout much of the South.

The South

In Dixie, where the Birch Society has 19 full-time paid coordinators, the growth of the Society closely parallels the growth of the new Republican Party which sprang full-blown on the Southern scene in the 1964 election on the crest of the Goldwater tide. Birchers have made themselves a factor in the new Republican strength in at least six of the 11 states of the Old Confederacy — Alabama, Georgia, Florida, Louisiana, Mississippi and Louisiana. All went for Goldwater in 1964 except Florida.

Birch members have insinuated themselves into a number of local GOP positions in Alabama and Georgia and have close ties to the party in the other four states.

Some GOP leaders in the South have personally encouraged the support of the Society because, as Los Angeles *Times* reporter Jack Nelson noted in a September, 1965, survey, "the party of Lincoln has become the party of the white man in much of Dixie." Elements of the new Republican Party in the South and the Birch Society have emerged as a major anti-civil rights and pro-segregationist force on the Southern scene, replacing the declining White Citizens Councils as the spearhead of the non-violent opposition to civil rights.

Of all the Southern states, the Birch Society is strongest

in Alabama. J. W. (Red) Gandy, an influential Republican and a volunteer coordinator for the Society, was quoted by Nelson of the Los Angeles *Times* as declaring: "The Birch Society is the strongest conservative organization in the State — stronger than both political parties."

Gandy denied — as too high — reports that there are several hundred Birch chapters in Alabama. But, he said, there are some 95 chapters in Birmingham which had signed a full-page ad in the Birmingham *News* and pointed to other Birchite strength in Mobile, Montgomery and Huntsville.

John Grenier, executive director of the GOP National Committee in the 1964 campaign and a Republican leader in Alabama, acknowledged the strength of the Birch Society and declared:

> "They worked for the Republican Party in the past and I trust they'll work for the Republican Party in the future. But I have told them that their first allegiance is to the party's principles rather than to the John Birch Society and they understand the wisdom of that."

Craig Knowles, finance director of the Alabama GOP, paid tribute to the zealousness and dedication of Birchites in the party: "You get a Birch member who's loyal to the party and he'll donate money and work for the party day and night."

N. Floyd McGowin, Sr., a wealthy lumber dealer from Chapman, is a member of the Birch Society National Council and was an alternate delegate to the 1964 Republican National Convention.

Despite the strength of the Birchers in Alabama, and the role they fixed for themselves in the GOP there, Grenier said the number of Society members holding positions of power in the state party organization was "not substantial."

The Los Angeles *Times* survey also reported that in several Georgia counties, the leadership of the Republican Party and that of the John Birch Society are almost identical, and that a number of physicians took leadership roles in both groups during 1964 as a means of fighting Medicare. The Society is especially strong in South Georgia where Goldwater ran up huge margins in 1964, and where young Howard Callaway became the first Georgia Republican Congressman since the Reconstruction.

81

The Georgia Chairman's Statement

G. Paul Jones, Jr., Georgia State GOP Chairman, said last October that the GOP there cannot afford to spurn the support of the John Birch Society. Jones made his statement at a news conference, a scant week after Morton, Dirksen and Rep. Ford declared in Washington that there was no place in the GOP for Society members.

Jones said that "instead of trying to run people out, we ought to try to bring them in. We're going to try to take care of everybody who wants to vote Republican." He said that as a minority party in Georgia — and throughout the nation — the GOP could not afford to do without any of the support it has. He added that no Birch members held state GOP leadership positions in Georgia, but explained: "There may be some serving as county chairmen."

Jones was also quoted as having declared:

"Although there are active and loyal workers in Republican politics who also belong to the Birch Society, there have been no indications that Republican activities have been in any way adversely affected by their membership in any other organization. I'm equally sure that their membership in other organizations have not been adversely affected by their Republican participation."

In Louisiana and Mississippi, Birch Society members are also working in the Republican Party.

Rousselot commented to the Los Angeles *Times* on the Birchite position in the South:

"We're very strong in Florida, Alabama, Georgia, the Carolinas, Louisiana and Texas. We have strength in Arkansas and Virginia. We're not so strong in Tennessee."

In short, the Birch Society has made inroads into the new Republican Party in Dixie and their gains there contain the seeds of a first-class dilemma for the national Republican Party. Reading Birchers out of the Republican Party would come just at the time when the Republicans are challenging the long-entrenched Democrats for the first time in the South. A Republican stand for civil rights, that would help in the North and West, would damage the party in the South.

9   *The Birch Map*

Highlights

By January, 1966, the estimated Birch membership in California stood at some 12,000 to 15,000, organized in perhaps 1200 chapters — a substantial gain from the estimated 700 chapters and 10,000 members which the Society could boast in California in mid-1964, just before the Republican national convention. With 16 paid, full-time organizers and some 200 section leaders, California has remained the banner Birchite state.

In 1965, New Jersey membership quadrupled with well over 100 chapters, serviced by four full-time coordinators. Indiana reported 40 chapters in the Indianapolis area, 15 in the Evansville area, substantial strength in Fort Wayne, and a network of chapters functioning in surrounding areas. In the area of Atlanta, Georgia, the Society jumped from 15 chapters in 1964 to perhaps 35 or 40 late in 1965, with Birch chapters functioning in all major cities of the state. Birchers, likewise, were active at the community level in Georgia. They sponsored numerous public meetings, often through front groups, at which Radical Rightist speakers were featured. And they sought positions of influence in PTAs.

Birchite growth in Alabama, with three full-time organizers, was likewise substantial, with a reported 100 chapters in the Birmingham area and pockets of strength in Mobile, Montgomery and Huntsville. In Arizona, Birch strength grew to about 100 chapters — enough to boast three full-time coordinators. In Texas, Birch membership continued at a high level, with several thousand members reported in the Houston area, another 1500 in Dallas and a pocket of Panhandle strength in Amarillo. Texas boasts a unique Birch phenomenon — several teen-age chapters in five Houston high schools.

In the Maryland-District of Columbia area, the Birch Society made marked gains during 1965 and members are now operating four bookstores, two "bookmobiles," a speakers bureau, and at least three stations of "Let Freedom Ring," the Radical Rightist telephone propaganda apparatus.

Late in 1965, North Dakota suddenly emerged as a center of great growth and intensive recruiting by the Society. Elsewhere across the country, there are other areas of expansion: Philadelphia and vicinity; Detroit; suburban Chicago; and Spokane, among them.

Greater New York, especially Long Island and Westchester, also shows substantial gains during 1965, spreading into nearby Bergen and Passaic counties in New Jersey, Rockland County, N.Y., and Fairfield County, Conn. — all further evidence of the strongly suburban character of the Birch membership.

A glance at the Birch map shows the distribution of Society strength across the country.

New England

• In New England, where the Society has its national headquarters, the number of chapters has grown to perhaps 70 or 75 — more than triple the number at the start of 1965.

Massachusetts grew from four or five chapters in 1964 to more than 30 by the end of 1965. Major strength was centered in the southeastern part of the state and in the suburbs of Greater Boston.

Rhode Island has doubled the number of its chapters — to twelve — since January, 1965.

In Connecticut, where membership jumped 20% in the two weeks following Election Day, 1964, there are at least a dozen chapters. What the Society lacks numerically in the Nutmeg State is more than made up by the intense activity of the members. They have opened several Birch bookstores and hold frequent meetings where the public is invited to hear Birch and Radical Right speakers. Many of these meetings are held under the auspices of Birch Society front groups, which have grown rapidly in Connecticut.

New Hampshire is the scene of intense Birch Society activity — mainly centered, as already described, around Nashua and the nearby communities of Hudson, Derry, Hollis, Milford and Amherst.

Maine and Vermont have hardly been dented by the Society but Maine is a prime target of the Society's organizing efforts.

The South

• In the South, aside from the Society's growth in Georgia and Alabama, there is solid strength in Florida. It is centered mainly in the Jacksonville, Palm Beach, Daytona, St. Petersburg and St. Augustine areas, and in Sarasota. In Sarasota, which is the headquarters of "Let Freedom Ring," the telephone operation, Birchers have had an impact on local school affairs, changing a moderate school board and sparking a movement that cost the Superintendent of Schools his job. There were also perhaps 15 Birch chapters strung out along Florida's northern boundary.

The Society has grown slightly in Virginia, especially in the Richmond area, has lagged a little in North Carolina, but has sharply increased its strength in South Carolina where assiduous recruiting activity has been under way.

In Louisiana and Mississippi, long strongholds of the now-declining White Citizens Councils, the Birch Society has made some headway. But both states appear to be fertile fields for Birch recruiting as Councils disintegrate. There are Birch chapters in several Louisiana cities and in all major cities of Arkansas, with several in the Little Rock area.

In general, Birch organization in the Deep South has been concentrated in the smaller towns and villages. Elsewhere, Tennessee has scattered strength with a concentration of perhaps 15 chapters in the Memphis area and organizing going forward in Oak Ridge. In Oklahoma, the Society is recruiting intensively and has made some impact.

The Midwest

• In the Midwest, the Birch Society has retained pockets of strength. Indiana, Ohio, Michigan and Wisconsin have for several years had enough chapters to make their presence known. In Michigan, Gov. George Romney fought a pitched battle with Birchers in 1962. While the Society's adherents there did not make banner headlines in the intervening years, there was little question that they were active. The same is true in Wisconsin, where Birch chapters are strung out along the shores of Lake Michigan northward from Milwaukee. In Ohio, the number of public Birch meetings rose sharply during 1965 and there are Birch bookstores in Cleveland, Toledo, Youngstown and Cincinnati.

Chicago, with 15 chapters, has been an area of disappointment to the Society. But recruitment has gone much better in such North Shore suburbs as Glenview, Evanston, Mt. Prospect, and Northbrook. Yet, there are four Birch bookstores in greater Chicago and a fifth in Rockford, Ill., which, with some 20 chapters, has for several years been a Birch stronghold. Early in 1965, the Society opened its Midwest headquarters in Glenview. There has been little Birch strength downstate.

In Minnesota, St. Paul shows vigor with some 14 chapters. In South Dakota, as noted, the Society made headlines when a Bircher challenged incumbent — and conservative — Sen. Karl Mundt for the Republican Senatorial nomination.

In Missouri, the Birchers claim a 100% increase in membership in the St. Louis area since the 1964 election. Birch strength until then had been estimated at perhaps 40 chapters. There are two Birch bookstores there. Other evidences of Birch activity in St. Louis are such front operations as "The America Wake Up Committee," "The Discussion Club" and an American Opinion Speakers Forum. There are also centers of Birch strength in Missouri at Columbia, home of the University of Missouri, and Centralia, the home of F. Gano Chance, a Birch Society National Council member and headquarters of the A. B. Chance Co. which exerts a powerful, if not dominating, influence in community life.

In the Plains States of Kansas and Nebraska, the Society, with 60 chapters, has tripled its strength since early 1964. Wichita, the home city of two National Council members — Fred Koch and Robert Love — is a center of strength and the home of a new Birch book store. Kansas City jumped to more than a dozen chapters. Birchers are active in some 30 cities in the two states.

The Society has pockets of strength in Iowa.

• In the Rocky Mountain States and the Pacific Northwest, the Birchers have made gains in the last year or two. Montana has perhaps 30 chapters. Las Vegas has about 15 chapters. Colorado and Wyoming have not shown any great growth but the members there tend to have an impact out of proportion to their limited numbers. Not much is heard of Birch activity in Utah and Oregon.

In Washington, however, the Society is strong, with chapters concentrated in Spokane and in Seattle which have about 25 each.

10   *The Apparatus*

Staff, Plant and Finances

The John Birch Society continues to enlarge its staff organization, its operation, and its plant facilities. The Society employs some 220 persons — more than 120 at its Belmont headquarters, some 20 in other area offices and some 75 field coordinators from coast to coast. Founder Welch, at the end of 1965, was meeting a weekly payroll of $40,000 — more than $2 million a year.

In two years, the Society's two area offices (in San Marino, Calif., and in Houston) have grown to five: a Midwest regional office in Glenview, Ill., just outside Chicago; an Eastern office in White Plains, N. Y., just outside New York City; and a special office in Washington, D.C. Late in 1965, the Houston headquarters was transferred to Dallas. The San Marino Western headquarters has tripled its office space. Late in 1964, the Society acquired the old Boston and Maine railroad station in Belmont — its national headquarters — for the storage of books. It has doubled its floor space.

By the end of 1965 the Society was spending well over $5 million a year. Add items for capital outlay and for local Society activity, such as full-page newspaper advertisements, and it is clear that Robert Welch achieved his goal of a total Society cash flow of $6 million for 1965. The Society grossed $1.6 million in 1963 and $3.2 million in 1964. Robert Welch's financial goal for 1966 is $12 million.

The Complex

The national organization which has already established itself as a unique apparatus on the usually-splintered Right is a vast complex of local chapters, hierarchies, chains of command, public relations men, publishing companies, local organizations, discussion groups, fund-raisers, Red-hunters, book stores, magazines, pressure groups and movies for recruiting purposes.

Under the Birch Society's upper hierarchy — the Founder, the Executive Committee, the National Council, and the coordinators — there exists a volunteer hierarchy of section and chapter leaders. Monthly, in the chapter leaders' homes, in quiet little cells of from 6 to 25 members (the average group is 10 or 15), the broad and busy base of the monolith meets.

Behind its efforts lies a corporate structure in which are found Robert Welch, Inc., The John Birch Society, Inc., the Belmont and Western Islands Publishing Companies, and the various enterprises bearing the name, "American Opinion."

There also exists a practical, energetic and permanent apparatus for recruiting and for the production and marketing of propaganda, and a nation-wide system of loosely-organized but tightly-orthodox front groups. There is a vast library of avowedly patriotic books, two Society-published magazines, a speakers' bureau, and hundreds of "American Opinion" bookstores.

The Magazine

American Opinion, the monthly magazine published by Robert Welch and the John Birch Society, sells for $1 a copy and now claims a larger circulation than any other political "review" in America. It is intended to be a molder of "Americanist" thinking, to instill in its readers a profound consciousness of the all-pervading Communist conspiracy allegedly stretching from the White House all the way down to the local town council, the school board, the town public library and the local pulpit. The monolithic orthodoxy of the Society itself does not extend to *American Opinion* and its writers are given some latitude to express varying and sometimes contradictory opinions.

The latest official statement of *American Opinion's* circulation and ownership was published in the December, 1965, issue. It showed a press run of 50,000 and a paid circulation of 39,605. The growth of the Birch magazine in the course of a single year can readily be recognized when the circulation figures are compared with those on October 1, 1964, when the press run was 32,000 and paid circulation was 25,761.

American Opinion magazine is owned by Robert Welch, Inc.; The John Birch Society, Inc.; Miss Olive Simes of Boston; the Excelsior Housing Corp. of New York; Miss Ellen Lovett, of Needham, Mass.; John Rousselot of Arcadia, Calif.; Thomas N. Hill of Gloucester, Mass.; Robert Welch of Belmont, Mass.; Willard S. Voit of Balboa, Calif.; and N. B. Hunt of Dallas, Tex.

Robert Welch, Inc., is controlled by the John Birch Society, Inc. and has been ever since Welch gave his stock in Robert Welch, Inc. to the Society in 1960. The Society is a Massachusetts corporation of which Robert Welch himself is President. Miss Olive Simes is a wealthy Boston spinster who has for some time been a supporter of Birch activities and who, for many years, has been listed as a contributor to the Christian Nationalist Crusade, headed by Gerald Smith.

The Excelsior Housing Corp. is a South Carolina corporation which is a wholly-owned subsidiary of Deering Milliken Inc., the well-known textile firm. Miss Ellen Lovett is Robert Welch's long-time personal secretary. Rousselot is the Birch Society's Public Relations Director, and Thomas N. Hill is Field Director of the Society.

Willard S. Voit is the official in charge of the Birch Society publications depot at Newport Beach, Calif. N. B. Hunt is a son of H. L. Hunt, the multi-millionaire whose fortune was amassed as an independent oil producer and who is the founder of the Far Rightist Life Line Foundation Inc. propaganda operation which conducts the Life Line broadcasts heard on some 400 radio stations.

Robert Welch is the editor of *American Opinion,* the magazine he founded almost ten years ago and which he formerly called *One Man's Opinion.* Scott Stanley, Jr., a young man active in Rightist causes before joining the magazine, is the Managing Editor. The Associate Editors are Slobodan Draskovich and Professor Revilo P. Oliver, who are members of the Birch Society's National Council; Francis X. Gannon, the Society's Research Director, and E. Merrill Root, long a well-known name in Rightist activities.

The Contributing Editors are Martin Dies, Sr., the former member of Congress from Texas who achieved national prominence as the head of the old Dies Committee which investigated un-American activities in the 1930s and 1940s; Medford Evans, who is also an official of the White Citizens Councils, and Professor Hans Sennholz, an ex-Luftwaffe pilot who now teaches economics at Grove City (Pa.) College, an institution of higher learning heavily endowed by the Pew family who are principals in the Sun Oil Co. (J. Howard Pew, a leading supporter of Rightist causes in the United States, serves on the Editorial Advisory Committee of *American Opinion* magazine.)

The Assistant Managing Editor is Marian Probert Welch, who is Mrs. Robert Welch and who devotes much of her time to helping her husband run the multi-faceted affairs of the John Birch Society and its related activities.

Besides Pew, the other members of the magazine's 17-man Editorial Advisory Committee include Robert Dresser, a Providence, R.I. lawyer; Charles Edison, former Secretary of the Navy and Governor of New Jersey; J. Bracken Lee, former Governor of Utah; and Ludwig Von Mises, the prominent Austrian economist who is a leading prophet of 19th century laissez-faire economics.

The Birch monthly is a glossy and well-written periodical, and nurtured by advertisements, mostly from corporations which support the Far Right or in which Birch leaders have a substantial interest. These include the Allen-Bradley Co., of Milwaukee, which repeatedly purchases a multi-colored back-page ad in *American Opinion;* the Rock Island Oil & Refining Co., Inc., of Wichita, whose principal is Fred Koch, a Society National Council member, and Spindale Mills, Spindale, N. C., in which Council member A. G. Heinsohn, Jr., is a principal.

Other advertising is purchased by organizations and publishing companies of the Far Right, and from time to time, by respected book publishers. But noteworthy is the substantial proportion of "house ads" trumpeting books published by Western Islands, the Birch publishing house.

On the cover of *American Opinion* each month, there shines forth a commercially slick portrait of an "Americanist" hero such as the late Syngman Rhee, the late Sen. Joseph McCarthy, or Ezra Taft Benson, or an *American Opinion* regular such as Dean Manion, Martin Dies, or Taylor Caldwell.

American Opinion has, Welch hopes, some 80,000 salesmen — all members of the Birch Society being constantly pressed to sell subscriptions and to persuade local newsstands and drug stores to stock a few copies each month. An offer is made of a handsome profit of 40¢-50¢ a copy, made possible by the magazine's high retail price.

Welch tries to shrug off Birch Society responsibility for the Society-controlled magazine whenever a writer runs to an embarrassing extreme. Welch claims he allows writers a sort of intellectual "freedom."

The Printed Word

Unlike many of the Society's allies on the Far Right — such as Billy James Hargis, Dan Smoot, Carl McIntire, H. L. Hunt and Clarence Manion — Robert Welch has put little faith in radio broadcasting for his "educational" programs. "From the very beginning," he wrote in the November, 1964, *Bulletin,* "we have depended on the surer, harder road of education through the printed word." And Welch's conviction is reflected in statistics:

By late 1965, the Society's printing bill was $1.5 million a year. It was publishing and selling books with a retail value of more than $2 million annually.

Welch also publishes a new pocket-sized weekly, *Review of the News,* a magazine containing a day-by-day summary of world news without comment and with little slant, except in the choice of items. Presumably subscribers can use the magazine as a substitute for daily newspapers, which the Birch Society views as heavily penetrated by the Communist conspiracy anyway. *Review of the News* includes a section titled *"Correction, Please!"* — items in the news, followed by the editors' slanted answers to alleged "falsehoods, distortions, and more subtle Communist propaganda of infinite variety, in newspapers, magazines and over the air."

With book publishing fast becoming the major activity in Belmont, the dollar-a-copy "American Opinion Reprint Series" is being replaced by "The Americanist Library," glossy paperbacks published by Western Islands. "The Americanist Library" includes "One Dozen Candles," a group of books viewed by the Society as "Americanist" classics and as essential introductory reading for recruits or applicants. The books, which come attractively packaged and boxed, are sold on a sliding scale: one to nine sets are $8 each; 1000 sets or more are $5 a set.

An insight into the size of the publishing operation can be gained from the fact that the minimum printing of each title in the "Americanist Library" series is 100,000 copies.

Titles in the "One Dozen Candles" series indicate the kind of required reading expected of Birch members before they are considered properly indoctrinated:

— "While You Slept" by the late John T. Flynn.

— "Seeds of Treason" by Ralph deToledano.

— "America's Retreat From Victory" by the late Sen. Joseph R. McCarthy.

— "The Whole of Their Lives" by the late Benjamin Gitlow, a Communist leader of the 1920s who broke with the Party.

— "Shanghai Conspiracy" by retired Maj. Gen. Charles A. Willoughby, Gen. Douglas MacArthur's Intelligence chief in World War II, and a leading figure on the American Far Right.

— "From Major Jordan's Diaries" by George Racey Jordan which tells of the author's belief that American secrets were handed over to Soviet Russia during World War II.

— "I Saw Poland Betrayed" by former Ambassador Arthur Bliss Lane — purporting to tell how American money, prestige and productive might were used by the Communists to enslave Eastern Europe.

— "The People's Pottage" by Garet Garrett on "the

93

Communist-inspired conversion of America from a constitutional republic of self-reliant people into an unbridled democracy of handout-seeking whiners."

— "The Kohler Strike" by Sylvester Petro — "the part played by labor bosses, whom the Communists love, in gradually destroying our great inheritance."

— "The Invisible Government" by Dan Smoot, the story of the Council on Foreign Relations which, the Birchers claim is the "invisible government" seeking to convert the U. S. into a Socialist state, and then to make it a part of a one-world Communist system

— "France, The Tragic Years" by Sisley Huddleston — "de Gaulle's role in the Communist program," and "why the Communists and their allies appear to be the only stable group in French politics."

— "Nine Men Against America" by Rosalie M. Gordon, described by the Birchers as "perhaps the most important on the list" because it purports to tell how the Supreme Court under Chief Justice Earl Warren has been "destroying every safeguard which might prevent the Communists from carrying out their plans" in the United States.

The Birch list of titles by Western Islands or other Birch publishing arms, plus books printed elsewhere but available through the Society, is a thick pamphlet. Besides "standards" of Far Right literature, the list includes some books by responsible conservatives, others by little-known extremists, and some legitimate classics such as works by John Stuart Mill, Adam Smith and Frederic Bastiat. Included, too, are standard Birch Society documents — the Society's "introductory packet," one on civil rights, a "special" Society packet, and a "Warren Impeachment Packet."

Of interest also is the availability, through the Society, of the "McGuffey Readers;" a line of children's books — "Living American Stories," "Childhood of Famous American Series," and "Beginning-to-Read Books" — all of which suggests that Birch parents are intent upon grooming a new generation of Birch moppets to carry on the fight years from now.

94

The Spoken Word

Although Welch has put his faith in the printed word, in January, 1966, he announced that the Society was launching a weekly 15-minute radio program to be entitled *The Birch Report*. He told his members that the time had come when, "with our emphasis on the printed word still unabated, we need at least a limited but periodical use of broadcasting media, even if for no other reason than the direct purposes of our Public Relations Department." Welch said Rousselot would supervise the program which was to be paid for by multiple local sponsorships, and Welch added, "in plain language, we are counting on our members throughout the country, especially those with businesses that can use local radio advertising to advantage, to sponsor this program in their respective areas." The program was to be pre-taped and mailed to sponsors or stations at $5 a tape. Welch said leading Birch spokesmen and occasional invited guests would be featured.

Because to a great many on the Far Right, hearing is believing, the Society was making a number of "Americanist" voices available to listening audiences even before the radio program was announced. Increasingly, the Society made audio-visual materials available and members were continually urged to start forums, lecture series, and study clubs. The following are relevant sections of that apparatus:

The American Opinion Speakers Bureau was started four years ago and is now directed from the Society's Belmont home office. This service, which Welch sees as "a powerful medium for reaching audiences throughout the nation," offers Birch Society speakers such as Rousselot, Tom Anderson, Revilo Oliver, Reed Benson, and allies on the Far Right such as Harold Lord Varney, Willis Stone of the Liberty Amendment Committee, W. Cleon Skousen, and George Schuyler, the conservative Negro newspaper columnist.

A more recent addition to the roster of speakers was Sheriff Jim Clark of Selma, Ala.

Target organizations to which the services of these speakers are offered include, not only Birch groups and fronts, but other Right Wing forums and, wherever possible, established civic, church, veterans and school groups.

Birchers had been urged, when joining PTAs, political clubs and other community groups, to seek the position of program chairman to control the selection of speakers.

Speakers provided by the AOSB are filling about 100 appearances a month, addressing audiences at meetings that spread from Nashua, N.H., to Pasadena, Calif.

The voices of Clarence Manion, Tom Anderson and Revilo Oliver, as well as Robert Welch himself, are familiar sounds at Birch meetings, study and discussion groups — via albums and tapes sold at Society bookstores. "One Dozen Trumpets" makes it possible for members to hear a full 18 hours of Founder Welch himself.

The Society provides a study manual and a suggested reading list for discussion groups and study clubs to enrich the curriculum provided by the recorded materials. Exhortations to form such study groups have become a standard item on the Society's monthly agenda of projects and the groups have become a growing manifestation in hundreds of American communities. Welch has also recommended the study-guide material available from the Cardinal Mindszenty Foundation in St. Louis.

The Birch Bookstores

The John Birch Society has found it advantageous to establish its own outlets for published materials. Robert Welch's "reading rooms that sell books" — generally called American Opinion Bookstore, or American Opinion Library — have served as local headquarters for Right Wing books, flyers, films, rally tickets, and bumper stickers; as meeting-places for Birch members, chapters and front groups; and as convenient recruiting depots for new members. The stores also serve in some places as local "stations" for "Let Freedom Ring."

In 1963, the Society's peak pre-election year, there were about 100 of these shops; today there are about 350. These outlets handle the standard Society materials as well as the output of Billy James Hargis, Dr. Fred Schwarz, Kent and Phoebe Courtney, the Circuit Riders, the Rev. Carl McIntire, Dan Smoot, and the Church League of America.

A development of recent years is the introduction of "mobile libraries" — Volkswagon buses which can be parked at street corners or outside Right Wing rallies. A New Yorker named Fred Lawrence, for example, brings his book-laden VW into the Wall Street area and carries "the truth to the heathen" armed with Birch propaganda and a New York City peddler's license.

Robert Welch has been proud of his Reading Rooms, but Society officials sometimes deny their connection with the official apparatus when faced with embarrassment over the appearance of anti-Semitic materials in the stores or a revelation concerning an unsavory individual managing one. (In a Boston store in 1962, an associate of American Nazi Party leader George Rockwell managed the enterprise.)

Nevertheless, the connections between the individually-owned bookstores and the Society itself are firm. The stores stock "recommended" materials, and many of these are ordered directly through Belmont headquarters — on credit. Robert Welch and John Rousselot have attended many a bookstore opening.

Carmine Saccardo, of Milford, Mass., a non-Bircher who took the "no-official-connection" claim seriously, told his story to reporter Bob Creamer of the Boston *Traveler*. Saccardo took over the ownership of Milford's Paul Revere Book Shop, and soon thereafter removed most of the Birch material from the shelves because it wasn't selling. Local Society members had tried to tell Saccardo what to order, and later boycotted his shop in protest against his displaying a picture of the late President Kennedy. Torn from his only market and saddled with a $4,000 debt, the well-meaning Saccardo closed up shop.

"My own friends were calling me a Communist," he declared, "and no matter what I said I couldn't make people understand."

Recruiting for Holy War

The John Birch Society is little interested in trying to understand the viewpoints of others. Birchers apparently find it more satisfying and less time-consuming to call them "Communists" and have done with it. The Society is quite energetic, however, in trying to make others understand *its* point of view.

One such effort was the release during 1965 of a new motion picture. "Presentation Film #2," produced at a cost of about $70,000, relates the history, aims, and operations of the Birch organization. It is not meant to replace the original "Presentation Film #1," a 150-minute Welch monologue condensing the Society's *Blue Book* into a far-reaching view of a conspiratorial, Communist-controlled world. Rather the new film is a supplement to the old, designed for prospects who have shown understanding and serious interest after viewing the original film.

"Presentation Film #2" runs 90 minutes and it looks at the world, both technically and philosophically, in sharp black and white. It insists that while Americans were dancing (Fred Astaire is shown) and golfing (President Eisenhower is shown), the Communist conspiracy was eating away at the foundations of the Republic. Then, Robert Welch, the hero, decides to mobilize resistance into a vast, patriotic organization to save the country. The resulting operations of the Birch Society are thereupon presented — from the headquarters in Belmont to the neighborhood chapter meeting.

During the summer of 1965, members and prospects were invited to pay one dollar to attend local "premieres" of the new recruiting film. Now, a free presentation is scheduled almost every night in the stronger Birch areas. The 5,000 chapters are each expected to hold at least one such presentation a month. Sessions are usually conducted by a paid coordinator or by a volunteer section leader who generally supervises anywhere from two to twelve chapters. After the film has been shown, they deliver a practiced pitch for membership. Birch staffers generally expect to sign up — sooner or later — about 25% of those who attend a presentation.

The new recruitment film has also been shown to audiences whose members might never consider attending a formal Society presentation. Showings of the film have been arranged before such non-Birch organizations as Republican clubs, and on local TV stations, as an educational film on

Communism. In many cases, of course, the offer of the film is declined by a target organization or an alert TV station manager.

Another device increasingly used in recent Birch Society recruiting drives is the newspaper advertisement. Birch Society ads are written and produced at headquarters in Belmont for placement by local Birch groups at their own expense. The ads, usually designed for a full page, appeal to good citizenship via the headline "Support Your Local Police"; to fear, via the message "What's Wrong With Civil Rights?," or to curiosity, via the caption "What Is The John Birch Society? — The Truth May Surprise You." The ads are usually a solid block of type.

The Society, however, has never solicited just anyone for membership. Welch seeks recruits with a potential for zeal, dedication and indoctrination to serve as a cadre for missionary work at the grass roots. The films and the advertisements are aids to recruiting along with the specially-designed recruiting packets. These contain samples of Society literature, a copy of the Birch *Bulletin,* a copy of the Society's much heralded multi-colored Sunday supplement which has appeared in newspapers in major cities across the country and, to be sure, an application for membership in the Society.

11   *Conclusion*

The John Birch Society today appears to be a permanent fixture on the American political scene — at least for the foreseeable future.

Whether it can be quarantined on the fringe of the American political spectrum depends in large measure on American conservatives. If they have the desire — and the will — to do the job, a housecleaning can be carried out on the American Right that would separate the conservative wheat from the Radical Rightist chaff.

If the task is undertaken, the job will not be easy. The Birch penetration of American life has already progressed into many communities and into the political party structure.

Its radical extremism, rooted in a conspiratorial concept of American history and of current events, threatens the democratic process and the democratic climate.

It claims to be the only effective anti-Communist force in the nation, but its leaders cannot tell a Republican from a Red and have forfeited all credentials and any claim whatsoever to anti-Communist expertise.

It aids Communism by concentrating on a fancied internal Communist conspiracy, thus diverting public attention from the real internal and foreign Communist threat.

It divides the nation by charging those who oppose it — and those whom it opposes — with being Communist dupes at best and Communist agents at worst.

It wages all-out war against remedies seeking justice and equality for Negroes, and it seeks to exploit, for its own propaganda and recruitment purposes, the fears, the tensions and the anxieties of Americans.

Its aim is political influence and power. Its ultimate purpose is to stop the forward march of American development and to repeal, if it can, the last thirty years of American history.

Its members have already begun to appear on the political scene. A few already hold office. Some are candidates. Its followers bore into the vital organs of political parties.

It has penetrated and influences some public agencies such as the police, local governments and the administration of public schools.

It seeks, through its members, influence in voluntary groups, civic organizations and other bodies which play a vital role in a free society.

It sucks in, each year, increasing millions of dollars for its divisive activities.

It is an apparatus, a radical apparatus, comparable in size and impact to the Communist apparatus at the peak of its power in the United States twenty years ago.

It uses subterfuge and semi-secrecy — including front groups — to carry out its work.

It has not yet tapped its full potential nor mobilized that segment of the American population which thinks as it does.

It is likely to continue its growth in the years that lie immediately ahead — until its actions produce firm reactions on the part of concerned Americans, consciously convinced that it is a menace to the nation and ready to defeat it in their own communities and in the political arena.

It is a by-product of the fears and frustrations of a nation in transition at home and in a protracted struggle with Communism abroad — a by-product of the "long twilight struggle, year in and year out" of which the late President Kennedy spoke in his Inaugural Address.

The American nation has survived and rejected the false counsels of radicalism and extremism in the past, and will reject the false counsels of the Birch Society because the overwhelming majority of the American people are neither radicals nor extremists — whether or not they agree with prevailing national policies of the moment.

What is of concern in 1966, and in the years ahead, is the damage the Birch Society can do to the democratic climate and process before the good sense and sober moderation of the American people lay it to rest and render it a mere footnote in the history books of the future.

101

Reading List

Bell, Daniel (editor). *The Radical Right.* 394 pp. Garden City, N.Y.: Doubleday & Co., 1963.

Cain, Edward. *They'd Rather Be Right: Youth and the Conservative Movement.* 327 pp. New York, N.Y.: Macmillan Company, 1963.

Chapin, Emerson (editor). *Freedom vs. Communism.* 48 pp.. New York, N.Y.: ADL, 1964.

Decter, Moshe (editor). *The Profile of Communism: A Fact-By-Fact Primer.* 160 pp. New York, N.Y.: Collier Books, 1961.

Forster, Arnold. *John Birch in Uniform.* 4pp. New York, N.Y.: ADL, 1965.

Forster, Arnold and Epstein, Benjamin R. *Danger on the Right.* 294 pp. New York, N.Y.: Random House, 1964.

Forster, Arnold and Epstein, Benjamin R. *Report on the Ku Klux Klan.* 40 pp. New York, N.Y.: ADL, 1965.

Forster, Arnold and Epstein, Benjamin R. *The Radical Right and Religion.* 14 pp. New York, N.Y.: ADL, 1965.

Greenberg, Martin, *A Short History of Communism.* 64 pp. New York, N.Y.: ADL, 1964.

Hofstadter, Richard. *The Paranoid Style in American Politics and Other Essays.* 315 pp. New York, N.Y.: Alfred A. Knopf, 1965.

Johnson, Donald and Eisman, Bernard. *The Far Right.* 259 pp. New York, N.Y.: McGraw-Hill Company, 1963.

Overstreet, Harry and Overstreet, Bonaro. *The Strange Tactics of Extremism.* 315 pp. New York, N.Y.: W. W. Norton Publishers, 1964.

Raywid, Mary Anne. *The Ax-Grinders: Critics of Our Public Schools.* 260 pp. New York, N.Y.: Macmillan Company, 1962.

Roy, Ralph Lord. *Communism and the Churches.* 495 pp. New York, N.Y.: Harcourt Brace, 1960.

Walker, Brooks R. *The Christian Fright Peddlers.* 290 pp. Garden City, N.Y.: Doubleday and Company, 1964.

Index

107

108

About the authors

Benjamin R. Epstein is national director of the Anti-Defamation League of B'nai B'rith and has studied and written extensively on problems of prejudice in this country and abroad.

Arnold Forster is the League's general counsel and director of its civil rights division, and has submitted to the United States Supreme Court numerous legal briefs involving fundamental issues of civil rights.

QUEENS BOROUGH PUBLIC LIBRARY

BAYSIDE BRANCH
214-20 Northern Blvd.
Bayside, New York 11361

B

All items may be borrowed for 28 days and are due on latest date stamped on card in pocket.

A charge is made for each day, including Sundays and holidays, that this item is overdue.

SORRY NO RENEWALS